Excel 2024 Charts

EASY EXCEL 2024 ESSENTIALS - BOOK 3

M.L. HUMPHREY

ISBN: 978-1-63744-140-4

SELECT TITLES BY M.L. HUMPHREY

EXCEL 2024 ESSENTIALS

Excel 2024 for Beginners
Intermediate Excel 2024
Excel 2024 Useful Functions

EASY EXCEL 2024 ESSENTIALS

Formatting
Conditional Formatting
Charts
Pivot Tables
Newer Functions

See mlhumphrey.com for Microsoft Word, PowerPoint and Access titles and more

CONTENTS

Introduction

This book is part of the *Easy Excel 2024 Essentials* series of titles. These are targeted titles that are excerpted from the main *Excel 2024 Essentials* series and are focused on one specific topic.

If you want a more general introduction to Excel, then you should check out the *Excel 2024 Essentials* titles instead; in this case, *Intermediate Excel 2024* which covers charts as well as a number of other topics, including pivot tables and conditional formatting.

But if all you want is a book that covers this specific topic, then let's continue with a discussion of how to create charts in Microsoft Excel. We'll cover how to insert and format any chart type as well as discuss the uses for specific chart types, including bar and column charts, pie and doughnut charts, scatter plots, line charts, and histograms.

Charts - Types

Okay, our next big topic is charts, which are yet another great way to visualize data. Sometimes taking a thousand rows of numbers and turning them into a pretty picture is truly the best way to understand what you're dealing with.

The way you build or format a chart is generally consistent across the various types of chart, but different charts are better used for different purposes, so I want to walk through chart types first, and then we'll get into how to actually insert charts and format them in the next chapter.

Let's start with a high-level summary for this chapter and then walk through examples.

Column charts, bar charts, and line charts are good choices for when you want to compare values using two different categories. For example, sales by store by month. The value is sales, the first category is store, the second category is month. I usually use these for time-series data where one of the categories is month, year, etc., but you don't have to. I could as easily use one of these chart types for sales by store for different formats (print, ebook, audio).

Pie, doughnut, and area charts are a good choice for when you're doing a "part of the whole" analysis. For example, total sales by store for a year. In that case, you want a visual that shows what part of the whole year's sales each store represented.

Scatter charts or histograms are a good way to visualize random data and look for patterns.

Okay, let's look at some actual charts now to help visualize what I just said. For most of this chapter the data table we'll be working with is this one that shows sales for four stores across six months and also includes totals for each store and for each month:

	A	B	C	D	E	F
1		Amazon	Kobo	Nook	Google	Total
2	January	$ 1,747	$ 353	$ 470	$ 65	$ 2,635
3	February	$ 1,616	$ 767	$ 445	$ 106	$ 2,934
4	March	$ 5,099	$ 420	$ 314	$ 1,132	$ 6,965
5	April	$ 4,596	$ 692	$ 140	$ 1,928	$ 7,356
6	May	$ 2,165	$ 809	$ 407	$ 1,090	$ 4,471
7	June	$ 2,502	$ 261	$ 244	$ 1,113	$ 4,120
8	Total	$ 17,725	$ 3,302	$ 2,020	$ 5,434	$ 28,481

(It's fake data so don't read anything into it or get hung up on if there's a weird number.)
First up:

Column and Bar Charts

Column and bar charts are essentially the exact same thing, it's just a question of whether the bars are vertical (column) or horizontal (bar). Excel includes both 2-D and 3-D versions of these charts.

In general, 3-D feels a bit gimmicky to me—like something that would be used in a bad consulting presentation. You do you, but if you're going to use 3-D, do it for a reason. (I do have an example of one possible use below and I have been known to be wrong before so there may be other uses out there.)

There are three main types of column and bar charts: clustered, stacked, and 100% stacked.

Clustered Charts

Here we have both a clustered column and a clustered bar chart that show the amount earned in each store for each month:

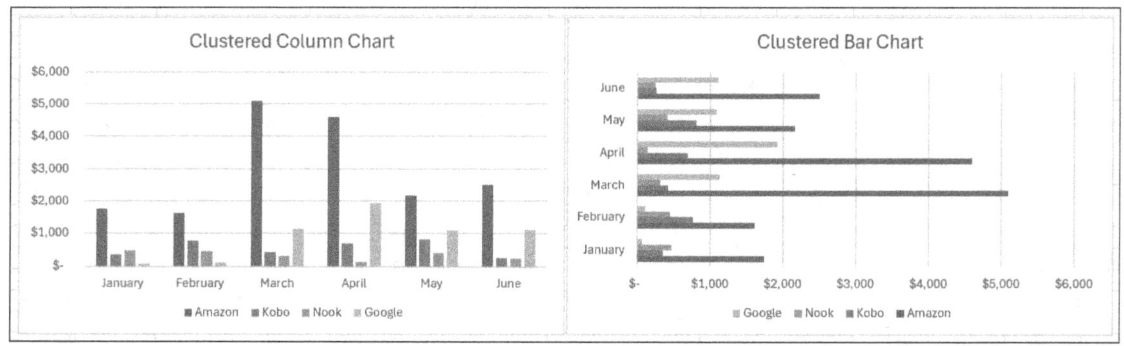

You can see that Excel created a separate column or bar for each store for each time period. The color of the column or bar stays the same for each store for each month, but the "height" of the column or bar varies month-to-month based on the sales for that particular store in that particular month.

Amazon, for example, is the darkest color. You can easily see that within each month Amazon had the highest sales compared to the other stores, but that it went up and down across the time period. You can also see that Google (the lightest colored column/bar) had a good month in April compared to its sales in other months.

Clustered columns are great for situations like this where you want to see the relative performance of a limited number of one category across a limited number of a second category. However, they can quickly get out of hand. Above, I have four stores and six months. That's easy enough to read. But imagine how busy this would get if I had ten stores across twenty-four months. It'd be a nightmare.

Also, note that it's pretty hard to see the *overall* change in sales month to month. You can see the obvious ones, like the increase from February to March, but what about March to April. Did total sales go up or down? It's not easy to see in this chart type. If that was something you needed to visualize, this chart would not be the best choice.

Stacked Charts

The next column and bar chart choice you have is a stacked chart:

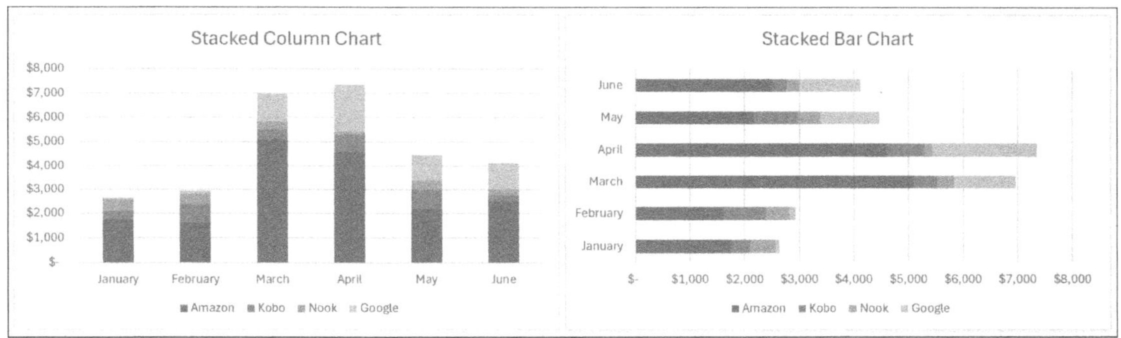

Stacked charts take the columns or bars used in clustered charts, and stack them on top of each other for each secondary category.

You can see here that instead of four separate columns or bars each month, there is one, and that each colored section in that one column or bar for the month represents the sales for a specific store for that month.

It's still possible to see relative performance between stores within a given month. But it can be harder to see how a specific store, like Google, did over time. Amazon is on the bottom so you can still see those changes month-to-month, but try matching up the sections for Kobo and comparing them to one another. Much harder to do.

The advantage to this chart type, though, is that you can easily see total performance across the time period much easier. Here we can immediately see that more was earned in April compared to March.

100% Stacked Charts

The next type of column or bar chart is the 100% stacked chart:

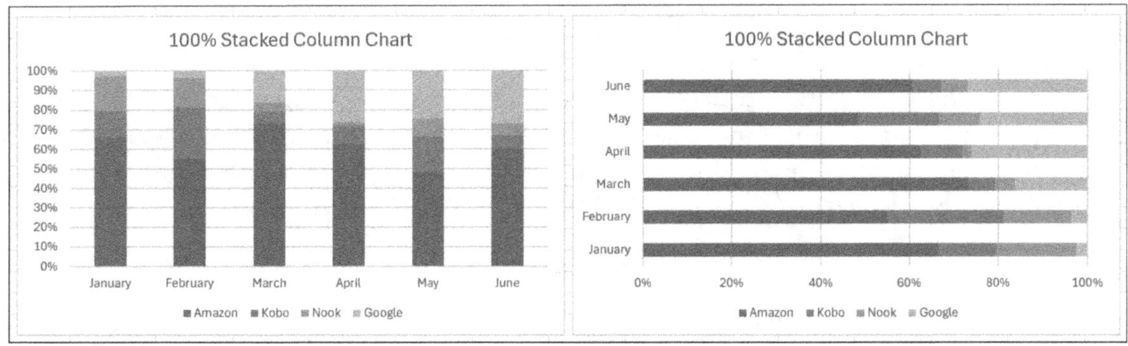

The column or bar "height" on this one is always going to be the same, because it always has to add up to 100%. In this case, the portion of the bar or column assigned to each store represents the *percent of the whole* for that store for that month. I mentioned before with pivot tables, that sometimes I'm not as concerned with total dollar value as I am with share of what was earned. Is one of my stores slipping so that even though my revenue is going up overall, that one store is in decline?

This chart type lets you see that better. Like the decline there March to April to May for Amazon. Why did Amazon's share of overall sales decline during those three months? Is this a good thing (I started selling better elsewhere) or a bad thing (my biggest source of revenue is in decline)?

I rarely use this chart type, though, because it can really hide key information. The problem with this chart type is that in one period you could have values of 1, 2, and 5, and in the next have 1000, 2000, and 5000, and they'd look exactly the same in the chart. If you're trying to pay your rent based on the amount you earn, the difference between making $8 in a month and $8,000 in a month is very important.

Same with disease analysis. Sure, it matters that Variant X is coming to dominate, but if Month 1 has 10,000 cases and Month 2 has 100, I think the 100 versus 10,000 is far more important than that the 100 comes 50% from Variant X instead of Variant Y.

3-D Column Chart

There is one type of column chart that is not mirrored as a bar chart, the 3-D Column Chart.

This one actually does provide information beyond what the standard 2-D charts provide, so I want to show it to you real quick.

The 3-D Column Chart is kind of like if you very carefully deconstructed the stacked column chart and put each piece that had been stacked one-by-one in a row behind the first piece. This lets you compare values for each store over time (left to right) as well as among stores for each month (front to back, back to front).

Here are two examples using the same data as above:

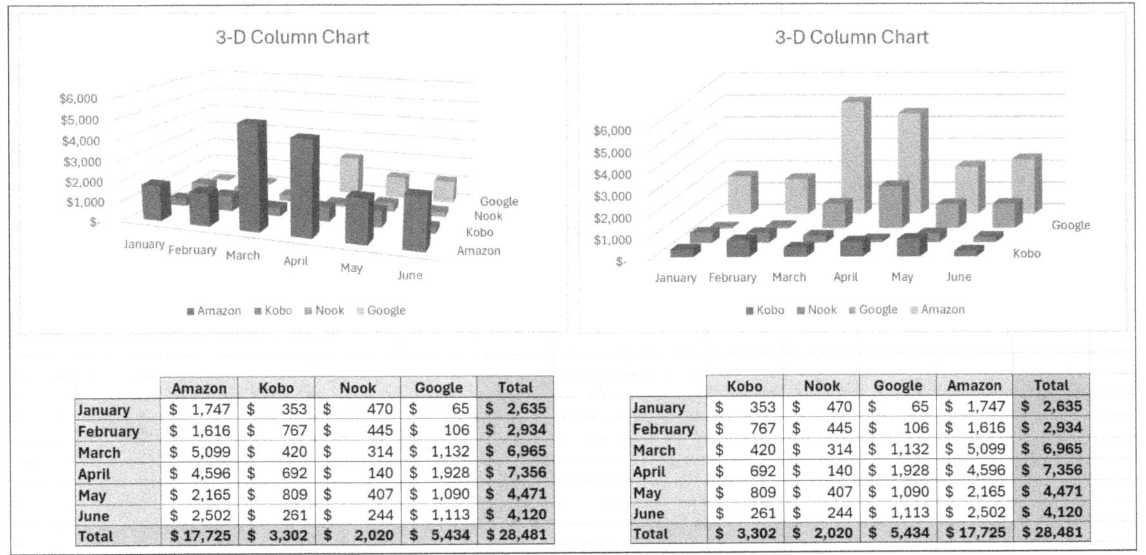

	Amazon	Kobo	Nook	Google	Total
January	$ 1,747	$ 353	$ 470	$ 65	$ 2,635
February	$ 1,616	$ 767	$ 445	$ 106	$ 2,934
March	$ 5,099	$ 420	$ 314	$ 1,132	$ 6,965
April	$ 4,596	$ 692	$ 140	$ 1,928	$ 7,356
May	$ 2,165	$ 809	$ 407	$ 1,090	$ 4,471
June	$ 2,502	$ 261	$ 244	$ 1,113	$ 4,120
Total	$ 17,725	$ 3,302	$ 2,020	$ 5,434	$ 28,481

	Kobo	Nook	Google	Amazon	Total
January	$ 353	$ 470	$ 65	$ 1,747	$ 2,635
February	$ 767	$ 445	$ 106	$ 1,616	$ 2,934
March	$ 420	$ 314	$ 1,132	$ 5,099	$ 6,965
April	$ 692	$ 140	$ 1,928	$ 4,596	$ 7,356
May	$ 809	$ 407	$ 1,090	$ 2,165	$ 4,471
June	$ 261	$ 244	$ 1,113	$ 2,502	$ 4,120
Total	$ 3,302	$ 2,020	$ 5,434	$ 17,725	$ 28,481

The reason I wanted to call this one out here is also because the order of your columns impacts the appearance.

In the left-hand 3-D chart, the tallest column is in front. This isn't because that is Excel's default. It's because Amazon was the first store listed in my data table, which I've added below the chart so you can see it.

In the right-hand 3-D chart, I moved Amazon's values to the last column. That put the largest values for each month in the back row and, I personally think, made the chart easier to read. Note, though, that it also changed the color assigned to Amazon and the other stores. That's because colors are just assigned down the line from first to last and Amazon is now last. (You can customize colors. We'll discuss that in the next chapter.)

Pie and Doughnut Charts

A doughnut chart is just a pie chart with the middle missing. I'd say pie charts are more of a traditional look while doughnut charts are more of a modern look, but it's the exact same information.

On the next page are examples using our data from above, that show share of total sales by store for the entire time period.

In both charts you can easily see that Amazon has the biggest share, and that Google is second. But note that these are part-of-the-whole-type charts, so you don't see actual values. You don't know if this is a chart of $8 in sales or $8,000 in sales.

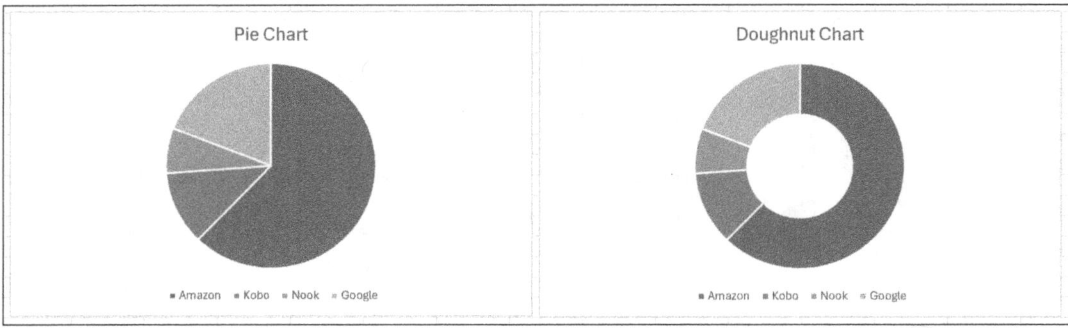

There are three other types of pie chart in Excel. One is a 3-D version, which I consider gimmicky. The others are a pie of pie chart and a bar of pie chart. I'll cover them so you understand them, but use them with caution.

Breakout Pie Charts

Pie of pie charts and bar of pie charts do the exact same thing, they break out a part of your data from your main pie chart into a separate chart. Here we have share of total sales by month in a standard pie chart, a pie of pie chart, and a bar of pie chart:

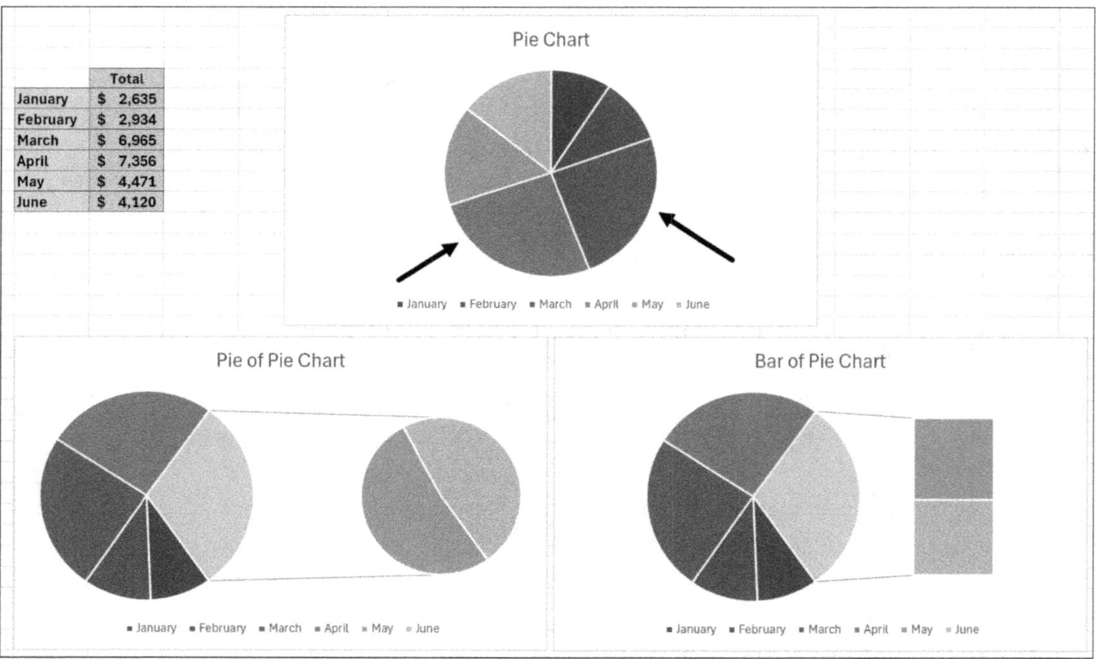

If you look at the standard pie chart, it's pretty easy to see that the two biggest months are March and April, the two bottom slices in the pie.

(In Excel you can hold your mouse over a chart element, like a pie slice, to see its label and value if you're not sure which color in the legend (guide) matches to that particular element. There are also formatting options to have Excel display labels and values on the chart itself that we'll cover in the formatting chapter.)

Okay. Now look at the pie of pie and bar of pie charts below that pie chart and try to figure out what you're seeing. It's the same information as in the basic pie chart.

If you just focused on the main pie chart in either one of those, you'd think that March and April, now on the left-hand side of the chart, are pretty much equal to that slice on the right-hand side, maybe even a little smaller. It would no longer be obvious that March and April were the best months because that third pie slice is just as big.

What is actually happening here is that the third pie slice there on the right side is a combination of two different months, May and June. And then that second chart on the right side, whether it be a pie chart or a bar chart, is just those two months charted against one another. (In other charts this could be many fields, but in this case Excel just chose those two.)

I do not find it intuitive to interpret these charts correctly. My natural inclination is to compare the size of the different slices to one another, which makes me think that May and June are the same size as March and April even though they're not.

The bar of pie chart is a little easier to understand, in my opinion, because it breaks that slice of the main pie chart into a bar chart, but I still think it's confusing because that secondary chart gives too much visual space to smaller values than it should.

I'm sure there are uses for these, just ask yourself before you use either one whether it helps explain your data or whether it causes confusion. If you're in a field where they get used often, most people will probably understand what you're doing, but if your chart has the chance to reach a wider audience, maybe find some other way to call out those smaller results, like a data table.

Also, these are good chart types to include labels with to help users understand what they're seeing. I have an example in the next chapter under Display Pie Chart Percent to show how I'd handle a pie of pie chart.

Line Charts

Line charts are great for seeing trends, but there are only two line charts I would recommend you use in Excel, Line and Line with Markers. The other line chart types Excel offers are stacked line charts like we looked at with column and bar charts, but they aren't intuitive. I'd avoid them and use area charts or bar or column charts instead. They're way too easy to misread.

Here is a Line chart showing total sales for each month:

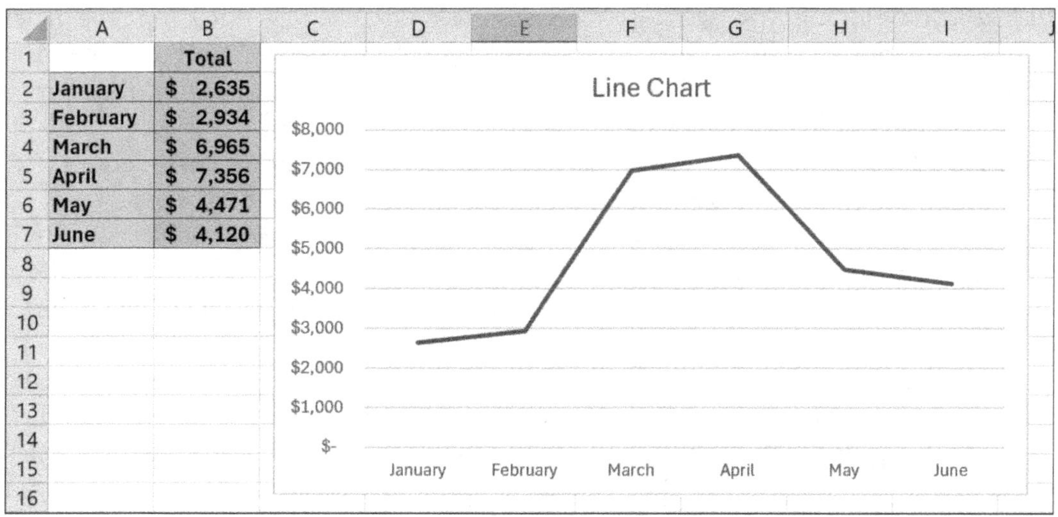

	A	B
1		Total
2	January	$ 2,635
3	February	$ 2,934
4	March	$ 6,965
5	April	$ 7,356
6	May	$ 4,471
7	June	$ 4,120

You can easily see how total sales were up in March and April, and how they stayed up a bit in May and June.

Here is a Line with Markers chart of sales for each store for each month:

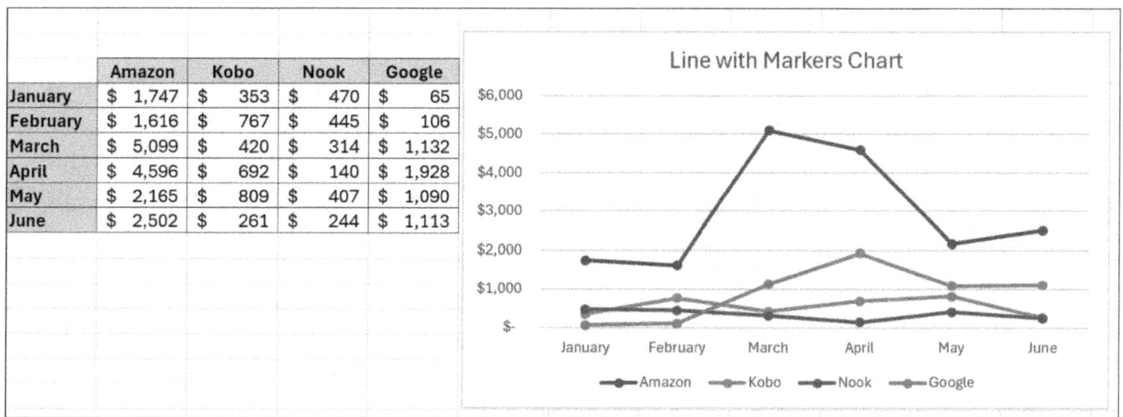

	Amazon	Kobo	Nook	Google
January	$ 1,747	$ 353	$ 470	$ 65
February	$ 1,616	$ 767	$ 445	$ 106
March	$ 5,099	$ 420	$ 314	$ 1,132
April	$ 4,596	$ 692	$ 140	$ 1,928
May	$ 2,165	$ 809	$ 407	$ 1,090
June	$ 2,502	$ 261	$ 244	$ 1,113

To include lines for each store, all I had to do was include the columns of data for the individual stores, Excel did the rest. The first column is the x-axis, the rest are charted against that.

Area Charts

We have all seen a lot of area charts over the last few years. Or maybe it's just me. A lot of the "share of variant" charts use an area chart to show which variants are gaining traction or fading away. Where the stacked line charts fail miserably, an area chart works. It basically creates a colored layer for each category where the width of the layer for a given period is determined by the value or percent of total for that period.

Here is a Stacked Area Chart and a 100% Stacked Area Chart for sales by store by month:

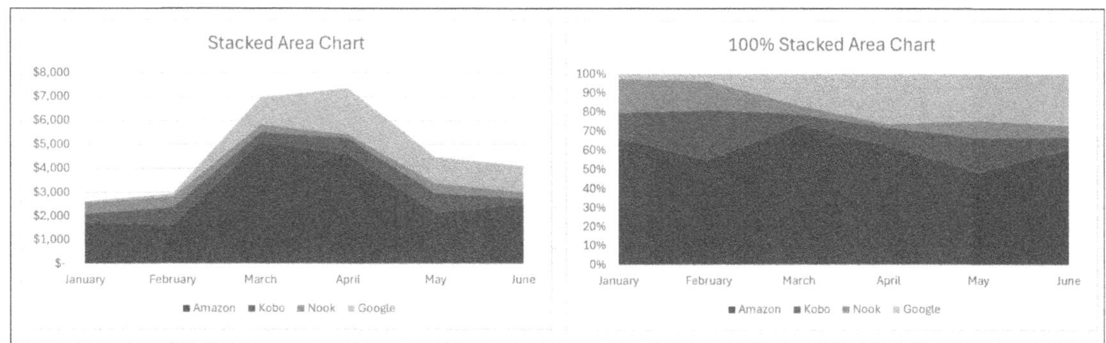

By filling in the space below each line, it becomes clear that the different pieces are stacked on top of one another to make a whole.

I think this chart type better shows the change for a specific store from period to period than a stacked column or bar chart, because even when a specific store is a small part of the whole, you can still see whether that layer gets bigger or smaller over time.

Of course, be careful once again with the 100% stacked chart since it doesn't show changes in overall total value. $8 and $8,000 can look the exact same.

Also, I'm thinking on this one that it's only good for time series data. I don't think I'd use it for sales by store by format, for example, because those don't really represent a continuum like time does. I looked online and found a few that broke that (like one that had car colors instead of months), but I think they were less successful than if they'd used a column or bar chart for that data instead.

Okay, next.

Scatter Plots

A scatter plot puts a dot on the chart for the intersection of two values. You can choose to just plot those dots (Scatter) or to plot those dots and connect them with a smooth line or a straight line (Scatter with Smooth Lines, Scatter with Straight Lines). If you connect dots with a line, you can also choose to include a marker for each data point (Scatter with Smooth Lines and Markers, Scatter with Straight Lines and Markers).

A scatter plot can be a good way to see clusters in data points or relationships between different data points. For this one we need new data points because a scatter chart is more likely to be used for random measurements of two variables than for the sales data we've been using.

On the next page is a basic scatter plot of nine data points:

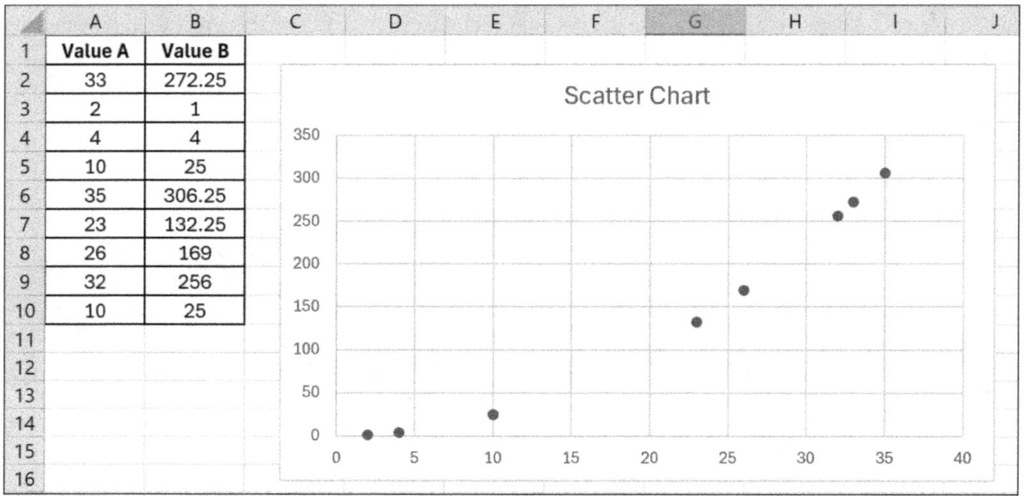

Value A	Value B
33	272.25
2	1
4	4
10	25
35	306.25
23	132.25
26	169
32	256
10	25

If I were to just look at the data in Columns A and B, I wouldn't be able to see that there's a relationship there. Maybe I could see that larger values of A also mean larger relative values of B, but that's about it. However, when I plot those values in a scatter chart, like I did above, suddenly we can see that there's a pattern there. Given the curve of that line, we also know it's likely exponential.

To confirm that, I really want to draw a line between those points. Problem is, if I do it with my data as it is now, it looks horrible:

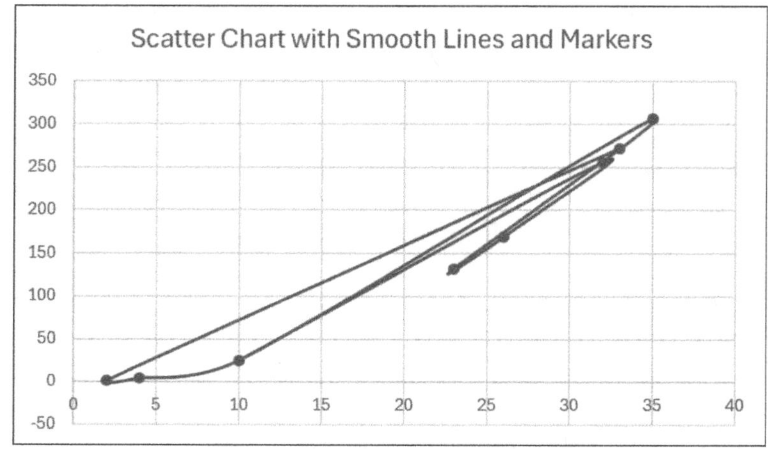

That's because Excel draws the connecting points between each line in order from first to last. It's basically assuming that there is a time component to the data you gave it, and that the order in which the data points were collected also matters.

If the order of the observations is not important, then sort your data before you create a scatter plot.

Here I sorted by the values in the first column and plotted again with a smooth line and it works:

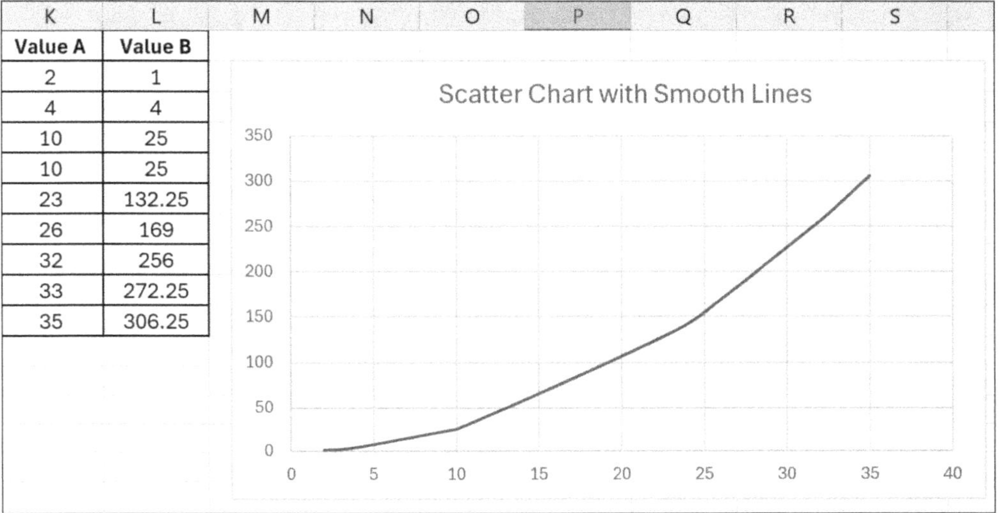

Value A	Value B
2	1
4	4
10	25
10	25
23	132.25
26	169
32	256
33	272.25
35	306.25

I can now clearly see a relationship between Value A and Value B.

With enough data points, the difference between smooth and straight lines becomes less important, but when you have fewer data points a straight line can more clearly show the lack of observations between two points.

It is also possible to have a scatter plot with more than two values plotted against the same base value. The first column of your data will be used to set the x-axis values, the remaining columns of data will then be plotted against the values in that first column.

Like this:

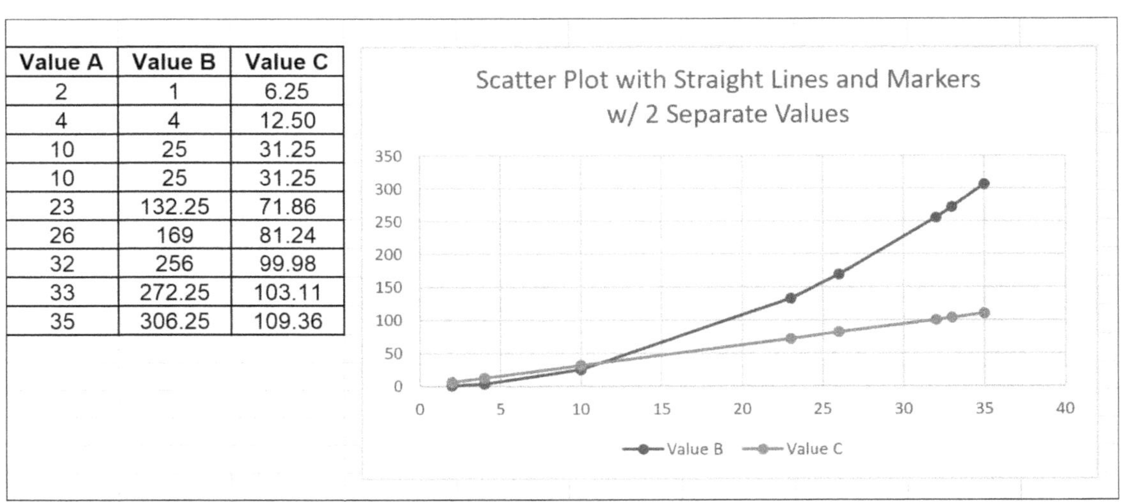

Value A	Value B	Value C
2	1	6.25
4	4	12.50
10	25	31.25
10	25	31.25
23	132.25	71.86
26	169	81.24
32	256	99.98
33	272.25	103.11
35	306.25	109.36

(You can do this without a line connecting the various points, but that might be a little hard to read because you'll just have a bunch of different colored dots on your plot.)

Bubble Plots

A bubble plot is like a scatter plot except you can have an additional value that is represented by the size of the bubble that plots each point.

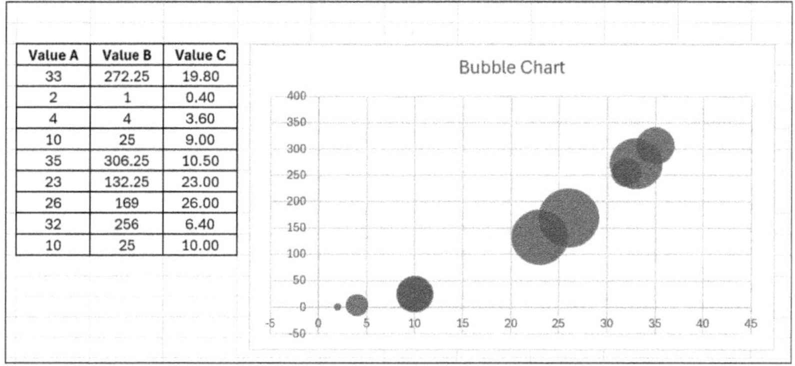

Value A	Value B	Value C
33	272.25	19.80
2	1	0.40
4	4	3.60
10	25	9.00
35	306.25	10.50
23	132.25	23.00
26	169	26.00
32	256	6.40
10	25	10.00

Histogram

Histograms take a set of values and place them into equally-sized buckets that cover the range of your data from smallest to largest. They're useful for seeing if there's a pattern to the distribution in your data. The more observations you have, the more clear any distribution will become.

Below we have two histograms, one with only 29 observations, the other with 100.

Both are using a data set that generates random whole numbers between the values of 5 and 60.

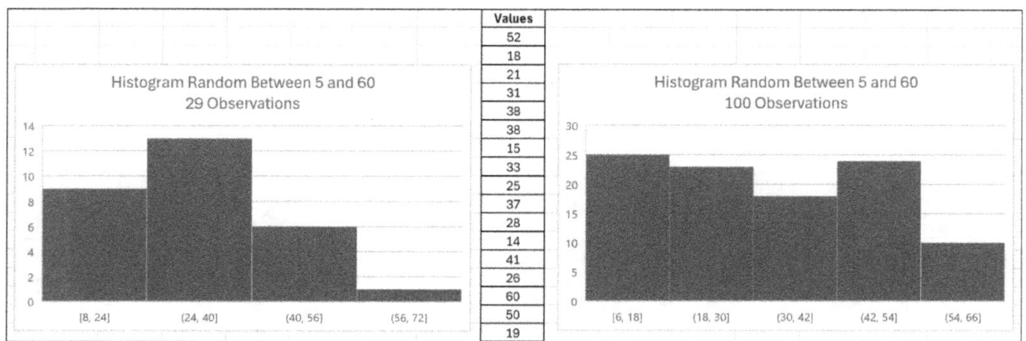

Values
52
18
21
31
38
38
15
33
25
37
28
14
41
26
60
50
19

You can see that as the number of observations goes up, the buckets that Excel assigns get closer to the true range of the values. Also, the buckets start to even out in terms of the count of how many values fall into each bucket. With enough observations, we'd be able to see that the values are randomly distributed across that range.

With normally distributed data, the more observations you had the more the histogram would start to look like a standard bell curve.

It is possible to customize the range and number of buckets Excel uses for a histogram. We'll cover that in the next chapter.

Other Chart Types

Excel contains other types of charts such as a Treemap, a Sunburst, waterfall, surface, stock, radar, and box and whisker charts. You can also create maps that are filled in according to various values. I'm not going to delve into those here because I think most of the readers of this book won't need them. Just know that they exist if you do. (And remember that Excel actually has excellent help available on the Microsoft website as well as through the Help tab if you have the right settings enabled.)

Combo Charts

This is also just a quick mention. Excel lets you create combo charts so that you can combine two types of charts in one.

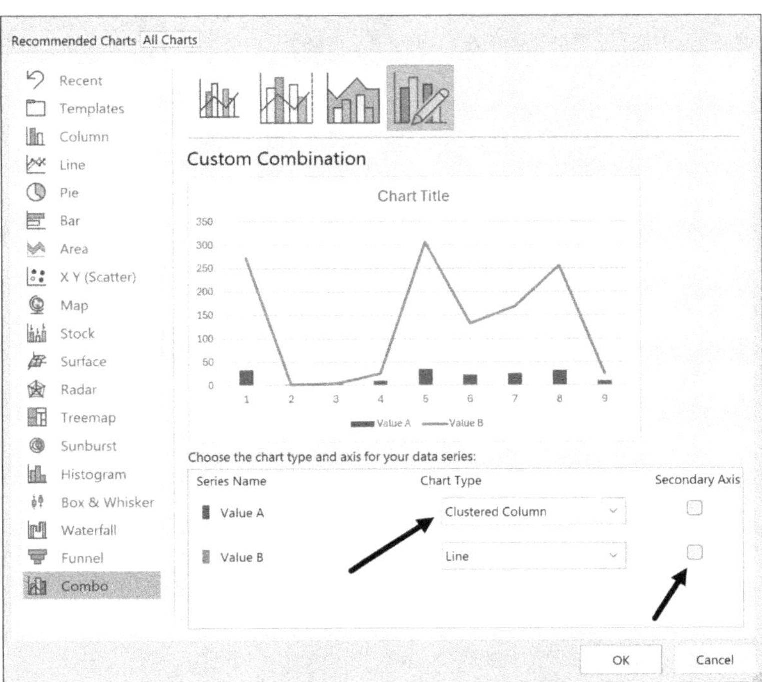

I was playing with this recently because I had downloaded a timeline template from the Office website and needed to understand how it worked.

What I figured out is that it was basically a line chart with values of zero paired with column charts that drew a bar for each point on the timeline. (Which meant that to get things lined up properly on the timeline I had to have my data points sorted by date, which was not obvious up front.)

It was a really interesting use of Excel. (That, me being me, I then expanded into using six different column charts so that I could color code different entries on the timeline.)

That's an advanced topic, though. Just know it exists if you want to try to go there at some point. And, if you do, use the secondary axis if your values are very different. (Like number of months and dollar value.)

Okay. Now that we've covered the different chart types, let's actually walk through how to create a chart and format it.

Charts – Insert and Format

Before you can create a chart, you need to format your data properly.

For column, bar, pie, and doughnut charts, you want to have labels across the first row and down the first column, and then your values in the cells in the table where those labels would intersect. Also, no subtotals or grand totals. If you do have grand totals, leave them out when you select your data.

As an example, this was the data table I worked with in the last chapter:

	A	B	C	D	E	F
1		Amazon	Kobo	Nook	Google	Total
2	January	$ 1,747	$ 353	$ 470	$ 65	$ 2,635
3	February	$ 1,616	$ 767	$ 445	$ 106	$ 2,934
4	March	$ 5,099	$ 420	$ 314	$ 1,132	$ 6,965
5	April	$ 4,596	$ 692	$ 140	$ 1,928	$ 7,356
6	May	$ 2,165	$ 809	$ 407	$ 1,090	$ 4,471
7	June	$ 2,502	$ 261	$ 244	$ 1,113	$ 4,120
8	Total	$ 17,725	$ 3,302	$ 2,020	$ 5,434	$ 28,481

For the bar and column charts, I selected Cells A1 to E7. For the pie and doughnut charts, I selected either Cells A2 to A7 and F2 to F7 (using the Ctrl key) or Cells B1 to E1 and Cells B8 to E8, depending on if I was looking at total sales by month or by store.

For the line graphs, scatter plots, bubble plots, and histogram, it was different. Those can work with one column of data. Put the label for the values in the first cell. If you want more than one line graph in a chart, or more than one set of data for a scatter plot, put the data in consecutive columns. The screenshots in the last chapter included examples.

Insert

Okay. Assuming you have a data table to work with, the first step for inserting a table is to select the cells that contain your data.

Next, go to the Charts section of the Insert tab, and find the dropdown menu for the chart type you want:

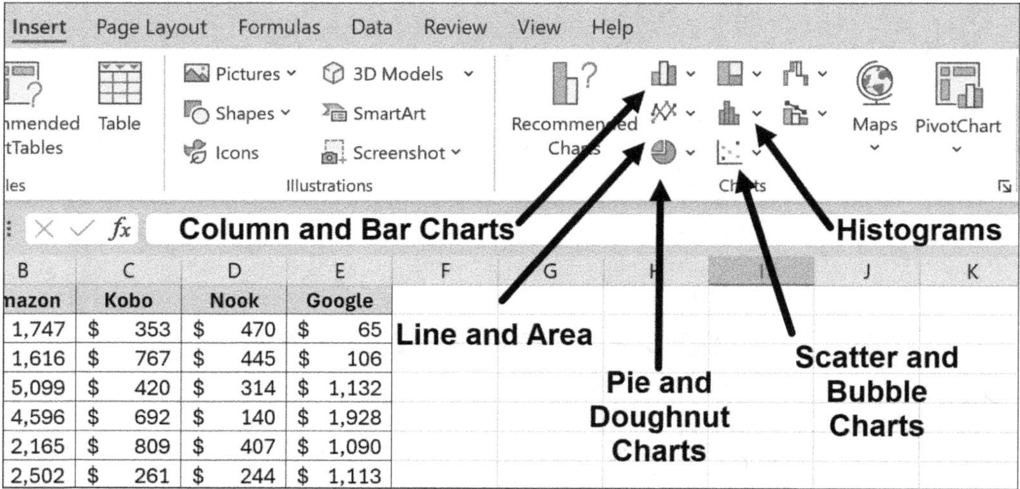

You can hold your mouse over each image on the menu tab as well as in the dropdown for each chart type, to see what kind of chart it is. This will also include a description of when it should be used. Here, for example, is the dropdown for column and bar charts where I am holding my cursor over the 2-D stacked column chart:

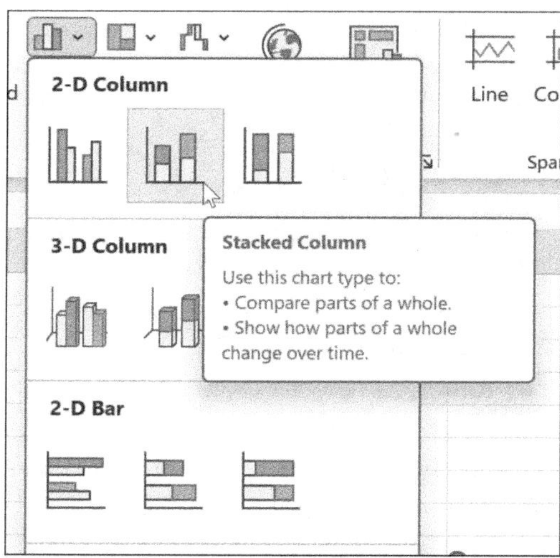

It says that the Stacked Column chart type is best to compare parts of a whole or to show how parts of a whole change over time.

If you have data selected when you hold your mouse over a chart type in the dropdown menu, the chart will appear in the background, allowing you to see what your data will look like. Click to actually insert it.

Another option, if you're not sure what type of chart to use, is to click on the Recommended Charts option in the Charts section of the Insert tab.

That will open the Insert Chart dialogue box to the Recommended Charts tab:

Click on the chart thumbnails on the left-hand side to see a larger sample of what your data would like like in that type of chart.

You should also see a description below the sample of what that chart type is meant to do.

Click OK to select the currently-displayed sample chart or Cancel to close without inserting a chart.

In that dialogue box, you can also click over to the All Charts tab at the top. That will show a listing of all the available chart types.

Click on a high-level chart type on the left, and then click on the icon for a specific chart type along the top, to see samples of what your data will look like using that specific chart type.

Here I've selected Bar on the left-hand side and Clustered Bar at the top:

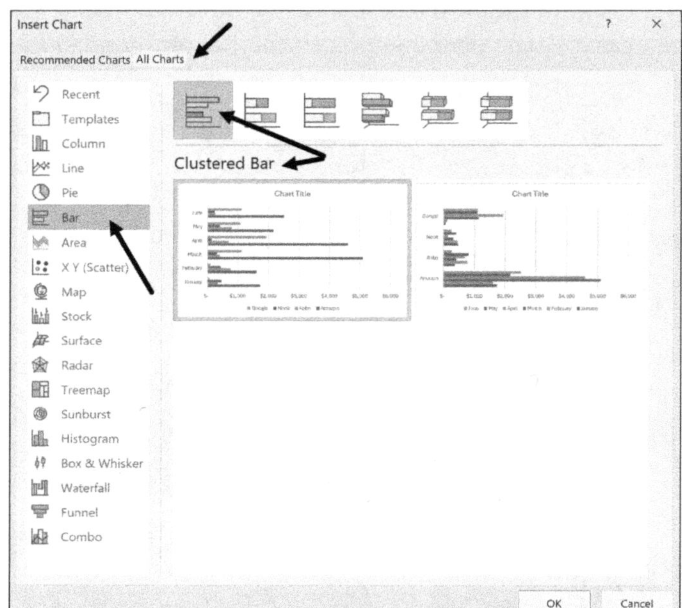

If you look at the sample charts in the All Charts section of the dialogue box, when there are two sample charts, like above, the left-hand image is usually how the chart will look with your data table formatted as is. The right-hand image is how the chart will look if you switch your row and column data.

In the image above, for example, the left-hand chart is sales by store by month and the right-hand chart is sales by month by store. (As we'll discuss soon, you can always switch row and column data after you insert a chart, too.)

Chart Menu Tabs

When you insert a chart into Excel and are clicked onto that chart, there will be two additional menu tabs available, Chart Design and Format.

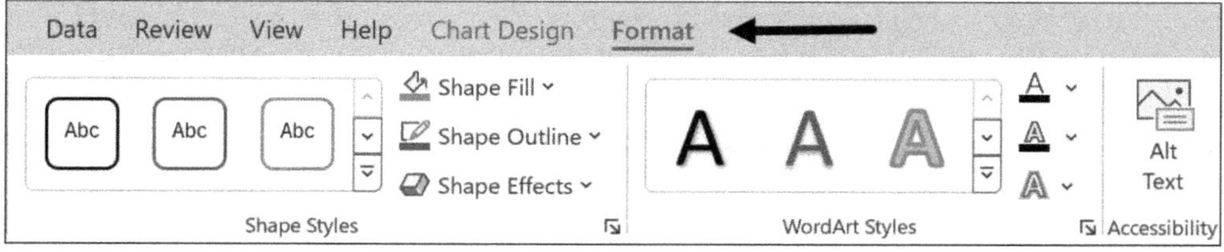

Chart Design is where you can choose the various chart elements for your chart, change your chart colors (like I've been doing throughout to make this print better in black and white), choose various suggested chart styles or layouts, switch your column and row data, change what data is being used in your chart, and change your chart type.

The Format tab is where you can manually change the formatting of your chart, such as the size or colors of different elements.

Chart Task Pane

It won't automatically be visible when you insert a chart, but there is also a chart task pane that will allow you to apply various formatting to the elements in your chart. We'll cover some of what you can do there, and how to open it, towards the end of this chapter.

* * *

Okay. Let's start talking about how to edit an existing chart. First up, all the ways you can fix an error if you didn't quite get it right when you inserted your chart.

Switch Row/Column

Here is a chart I just inserted in Excel:

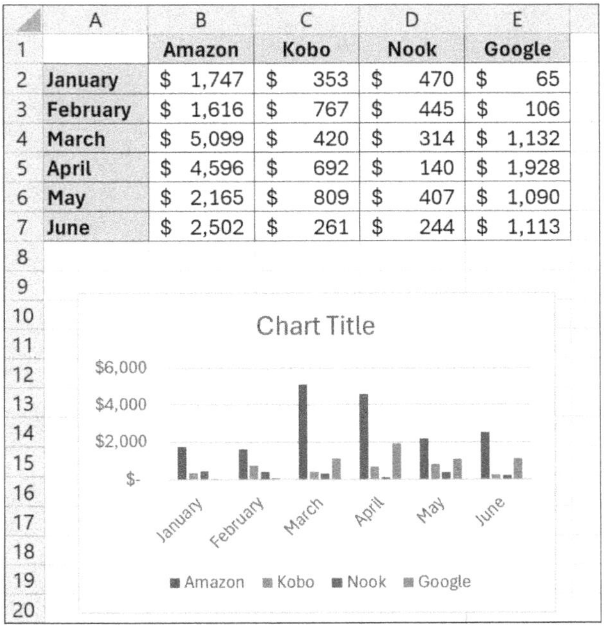

	Amazon	Kobo	Nook	Google
January	$ 1,747	$ 353	$ 470	$ 65
February	$ 1,616	$ 767	$ 445	$ 106
March	$ 5,099	$ 420	$ 314	$ 1,132
April	$ 4,596	$ 692	$ 140	$ 1,928
May	$ 2,165	$ 809	$ 407	$ 1,090
June	$ 2,502	$ 261	$ 244	$ 1,113

It shows sales by store for each month. But what if I had actually wanted sales by month for each store?

The easiest way to make that change is to go to the Data section of the Chart Design tab, and click on Switch Row/Column. Immediately, I get this:

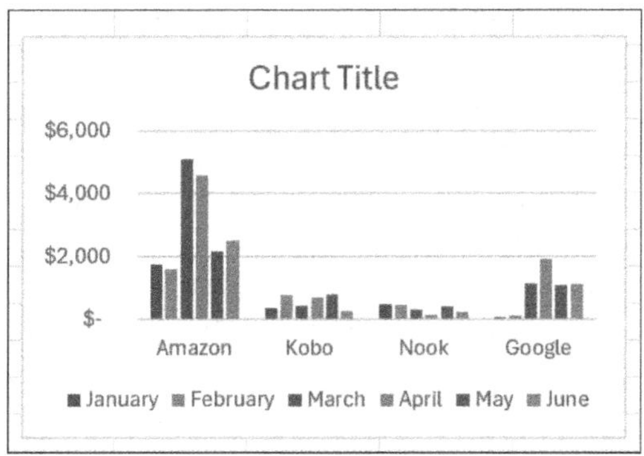

See how the axis is now the store names and the columns are now the months?

Change Data

What if you realize that you included fields in your chart that you didn't want to (like totals or subtotals), or you add more data after the fact and want to incorporate it?

For example, here I've added one more "store", Other.

	A	B	C	D	E	F
1		Amazon	Kobo	Nook	Google	Other
2	January	$ 1,747	$ 353	$ 470	$ 65	$ 50
3	February	$ 1,616	$ 767	$ 445	$ 106	$ 34
4	March	$ 5,099	$ 420	$ 314	$ 1,132	$ 123
5	April	$ 4,596	$ 692	$ 140	$ 1,928	$ 65
6	May	$ 2,165	$ 809	$ 407	$ 1,090	$ 228
7	June	$ 2,502	$ 261	$ 244	$ 1,113	$ 185
8						
9						
10		Chart Title				
11						
12		$6,000				
13		$4,000				

When you click on a chart, Excel will select the cells in your data table that are being used to create that chart.

Above, for example, Cells B1 through E1 are providing one of the categories, A2 through

A7 are providing the other, and B2 through E7 are providing the values. But note that none of the cells in Column F are currently selected.

One way to change the cells being used, is to left-click and drag from the bottom of the cell range that's already selected. In this case that would be the bottom right corner of Cell E7. (You may be able to see the angled, double-ended arrow there, but maybe not because it's a little small.)

When you left-click and drag to expand the selected cells, Excel should expand to capture both the header row and the cells with the values in them, but if it doesn't, then just do the same for the cell(s) with the header row value(s).

Another way to change your data, is to go to the Select Data option in the Data section of the Chart Design tab. Click on that to bring up the Select Data Source dialogue box:

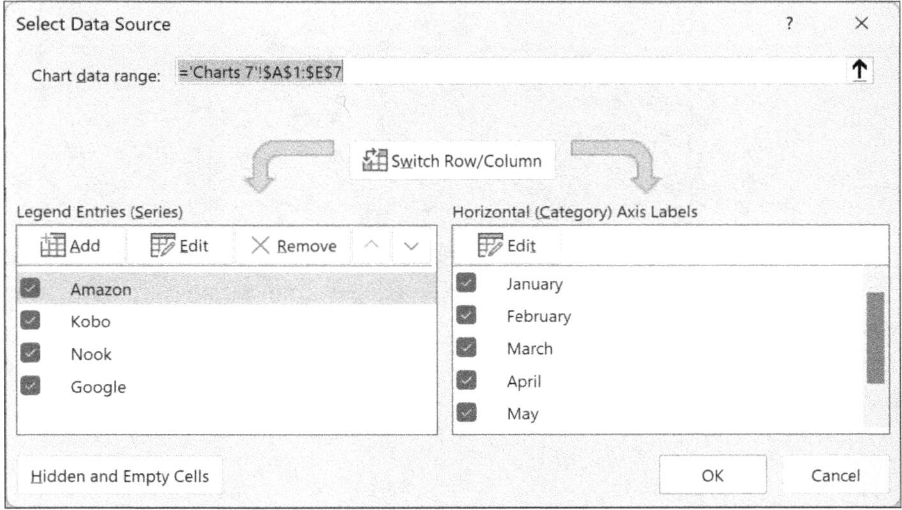

You can do a lot here, including switch your rows and columns, but if you're here to change your data, click into the Chart Data Range field at the top.

The Chart Data Range field does not work well if you click into it and try to use arrows. So one option is to click right next to the E, delete it, and replace it with an F.

The other is to select all of the text there now, delete it, and then go and select the correct cell range from your worksheet.

* * *

This dialogue box is also a great way to remove certain values from a chart after the fact.

For example, sometimes Amazon is so far out of range of the other stores for me, that having it in a chart obscures the detail for my other stores. When that happens, I open this dialogue box, and uncheck Amazon in the Legend Entries section on the left-hand side.

That removes the Amazon values from the chart.

* * *

This is also a place to go to fix the Legend Entries field names.

I generally recommend that you edit them in the data table itself, but sometimes that's not possible. If you need to edit them here, click on the value you want to change in the lower section of the Select Data Source dialogue box, and then click on the Edit option for that section.

This will bring up the Edit Series dialogue box:

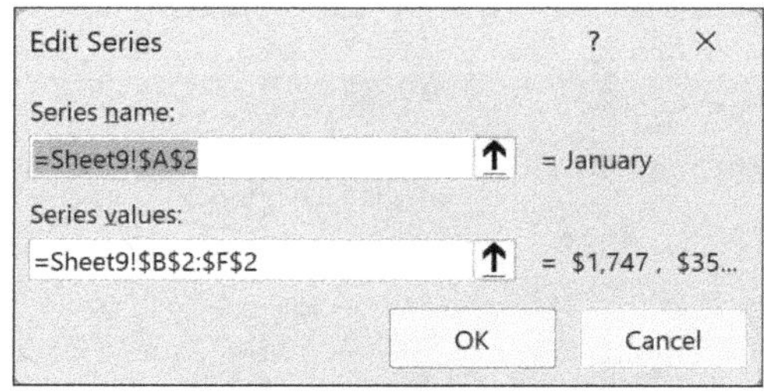

By default, the name fields will be cell references. You can see a sample value to the right.

For Legend Entries, click into the white box for Series Name, and type the label you want to use instead, and then click OK.

If you need to edit the Horizontal Axis Labels, that is a little different because it is a cell range, not a single cell. Instead of typing in one value, use curly brackets around your text, with commas to separate each entry.

{Entry 1, Entry 2, Entry 3}

For both, you can also replace the original cell reference or cell range reference with a different cell reference.

Use Cancel to close either of those dialogue boxes without making changes.

Change Chart Type

You can easily change an existing chart to a different chart type by clicking on the chart, and then using the Change Chart Type option in the Type section of the Chart Design tab.

Clicking on that will bring up a dialogue box that looks just like the Insert Chart dialogue box. From there, just find the chart type you want, click on it, and click OK.

* * *

Now that you have the chart set up the way you want, it's time to learn how to pretty it up.

Change Chart Title

If you've been trying things yourself as you read this book, you may have noticed that when a chart is inserted into Excel it has a default title of Chart Title. Not something you'll want to keep most of the time.

To change that title, click on it. You should see a box appear around the text. Select the text in that box by either left-clicking and dragging or using Ctrl + A, and then type the title you want.

You can format text in that box the same way as any other text in Excel using the Font section of the Home tab. That generally does everything I need for a chart title.

But if you want to get fancier, you can also use the WordArt Styles section of the Format tab to apply outlines to your text as well as special effects like shadow, reflection, and glow.

Another option for that is to right-click on your title box, and choose Format Chart Title from the dropdown menu. This will open a task pane on the right-hand side for Format Chart Title. Click around in the Title Options and Text Options to explore the choices available there.

Change Chart Colors (Easy Way)

To change your chart colors, an easy option is to click on the chart, and then go to the Chart Design tab. In the Chart Styles section, there is a dropdown menu for Change Colors.

Click on that to see almost 20 different pre-formatted color palettes:

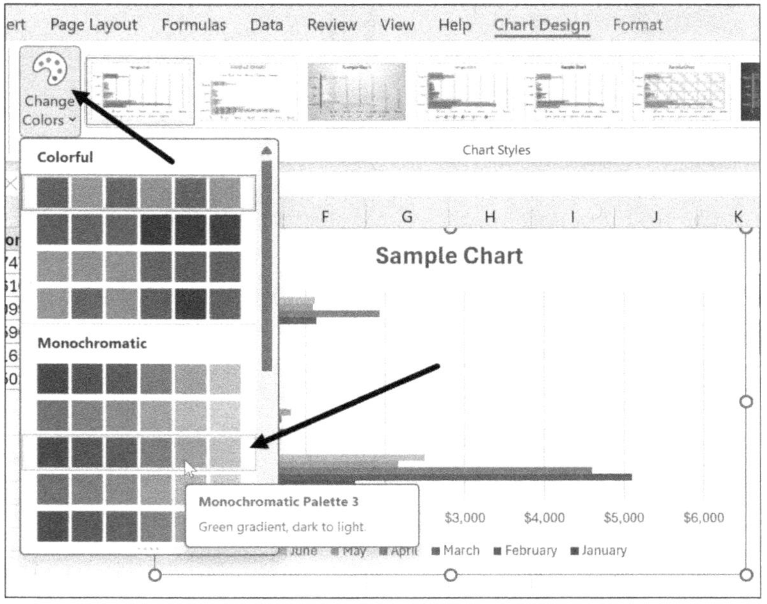

Hold your mouse over each one to see what it will look like. Click to apply.

This is especially useful if you're going to print in black and white. The monochromatic palettes ensure that different chart elements will be easily distinguishable from one another without relying on color difference to make that happen.

Change Chart Colors (Hard Way)

The hard way to change your chart colors is to do so one element at a time using the chart Format tab.

The first step is to click on an element in your chart. Here I've clicked on the blue column that represents April:

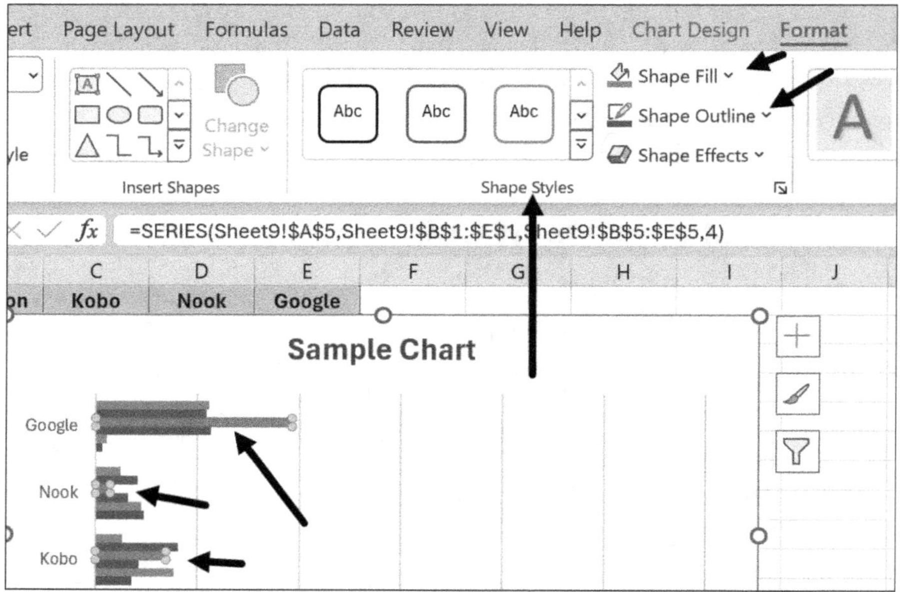

When I clicked on the first April column, Excel selected that column for each store. You may be able to see the dots on each corner for each of those columns. That means all of my April entries will change at the same time. If that doesn't happen, try again.

Once all of a specific element are selected, go to the Shape Styles section of the Format tab.

On the left-hand side are various pre-formatted styles. Click on the downward-pointing arrow with a line behind it to see the full list of options. Hold your mouse over each one to see what it will look like if applied

Here, for example, I have my mouse over a white shape with a colored outline in the first row, and you can see it applied in the chart in the background:

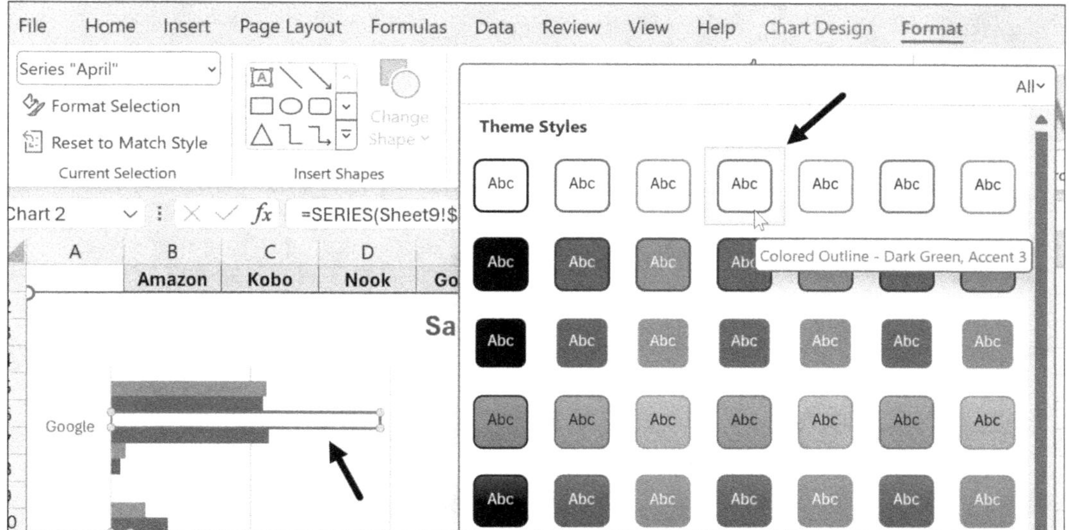

If you don't want to use one of those options, to the right of that are Shape Fill and Shape Outline dropdown options which will let you choose any color you want. (See the image on the last page.)

The More [Fill/Outline] Colors option in those dropdowns will bring up a Color dialogue box where you can choose other colors or input the values for a custom color.

For columns, bars, or pie slices, use the Shape Fill dropdown to choose a main color, and the Shape Outline if you want a different color around the edge.

For lines, use Shape Outline.

Shape Fill also has secondary menus for picture, gradient, and texture, but I would exercise caution in using them. You don't want your formatting to obscure your data.

Outline has secondary menus for line width (weight) and style (dashes).

Hold your mouse over each option to see what it will look like before you click to apply it.

It is possible to combine different fills and outlines for columns, bars, or pie slices like in the pre-formatted example above.

If you customize your colors, just pay attention so that you are keeping the colors distinct for each element. Pay attention to contrast between colors. It is possible to use two different colors that are so similar they might as well be the same, and that pretty much defeats the purpose of having distinct colors for distinct elements.

Change Chart Size

I often need to resize a chart in Excel. One option, if you know the size you want, is to go to the Format tab and enter values for height and width in the Size section:

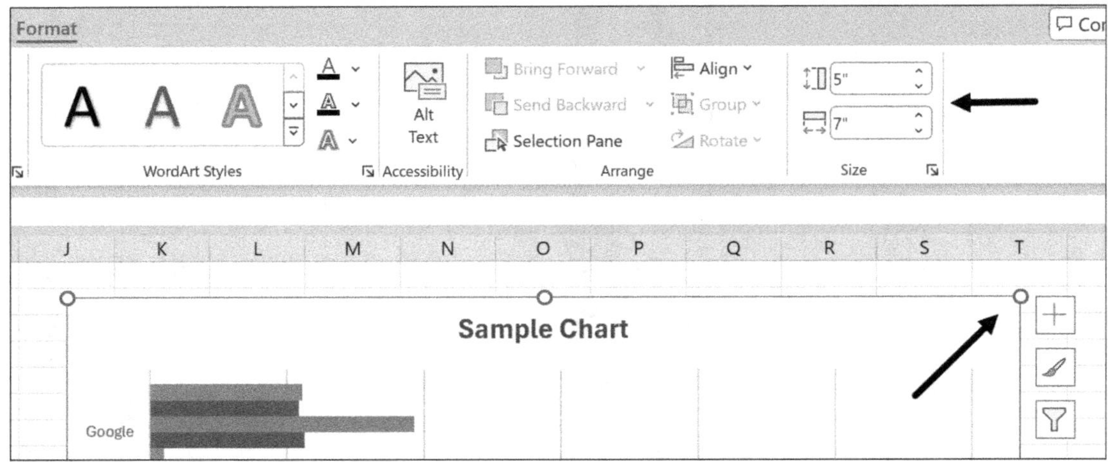

The other option, and the one I use most often, is to click on the chart, and then left-click and drag from one of the white circles around the perimeter. There should be one at each corner as well as one in the middle of each side.

You can see the one in the top right corner of the chart in the image above.

With either option, the size of the various elements in the chart should also adjust.

Chart Styles

Excel provides various pre-formatted styles for each chart type in the Chart Styles section of the Chart Design tab. They contain different colors, layouts, and effects, and will vary depending on the type of chart you chose, as well as any elements you've already added to your chart.

Here, for example, are some options for a column chart:

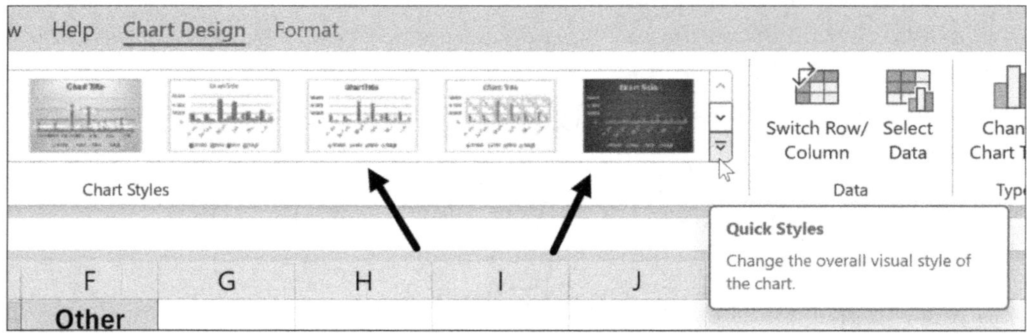

Click on the downpointing arrow with a line behind it in the bottom right corner to see the full set of choices available.

Hold your mouse over each one to see it applied to your chart. Click to keep it.

Personally, I don't think I've ever used any of these, but you should at least look at them once, because they might get you close to an appearance you like.

Quick Layout

Another pre-formatted option can be found in the Quick Layout dropdown menu:

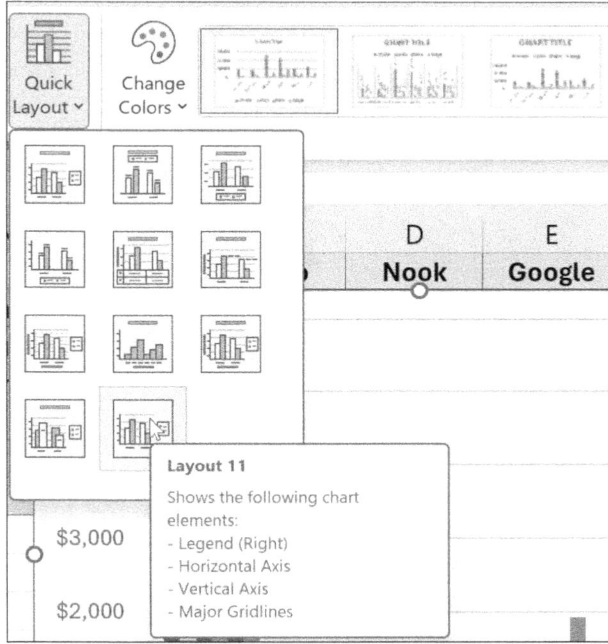

Quick layouts include different chart elements. For example, in the image above I have my cursor over Layout 11. Per Excel that layout would put the legend (that describes my values and their assigned colors) on the right, include a horizontal axis and a vertical axis, and add in major gridlines (which are lines that run across from the side to better help you determine the value that corresponds to a particular column).

Note from the thumbnail image that it would also remove my chart title.

Hold your mouse over each one to see what it will look like applied, click if you want to keep it.

Keep in mind that sometimes a layout will look horrible until you resize your chart to better display all of the elements. (Both here and if you customize your chart yourself.)

Like with chart styles, the quick layouts available will depend on your chart type.

It is possible to apply both a quick layout and a chart style to the same table, since quick layouts are primarily about what chart elements to include, and chart styles are more about the appearance of those elements.

But they do sometimes conflict. Where they conflict, whichever one you selected last will generally be the winner.

If you want to use these, you're just going to have to play around to see what you get.

Add or Modify Chart Element

At the far-left side of the Chart Design tab in the Chart Layouts section is the Add Chart Element dropdown. This is where I go when I want to customize my chart.

Click on the dropdown arrow to see the list of elements you can add or remove. If an element isn't available for a specific type of chart, it will be grayed out like Lines and Up/ Down Bars are here:

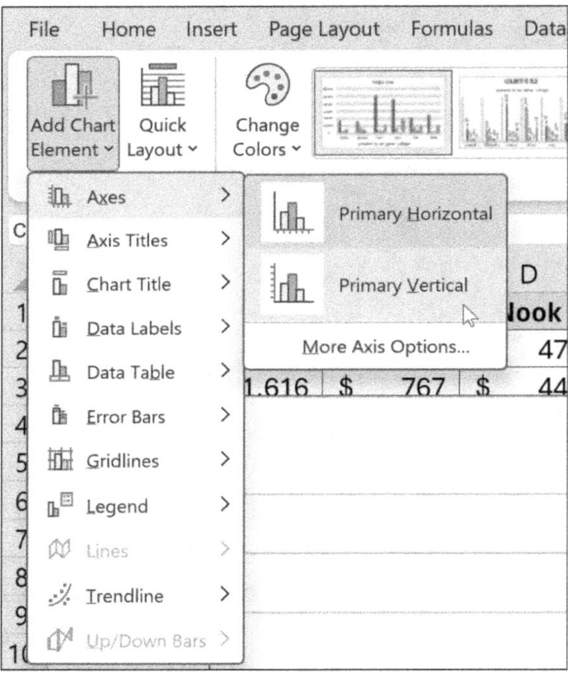

Each element has a secondary dropdown menu, like the one above for Axes, where you can see what choices are available.

Hold your cursor over each option in the secondary dropdown to see what would happen to your chart if you click on it. If the element is already there, clicking on that option will remove it. If it isn't there, then clicking will add or change it to that location.

Keep in mind for text elements that they can sometimes also be manually moved around or resized after you add them.

Now let's walk through each of those choices:

Axes

Your horizontal and vertical axes are what show the values. For a standard chart, horizontal is along the bottom, vertical is along the left side.

If you ever do a combo chart, it's possible to have a secondary vertical axis on the right side and a secondary horizontal axis along the top. The listed options will expand to also let you turn on or off those secondary axes.

Axis Titles

This option lets you add a text box to describe each axis.

Chart Title

This option lets you decide whether to have a chart title and, if you do, whether to put it above the contents of the chart or centered within the chart itself. I personally prefer to have it above, so all the charts in this book have the title in the Above Chart position.

Data Labels

The data labels option lets you decide whether to add the actual values to your chart. For me, I generally only like to do this on pie charts, because I use a data table with most of my bar or column charts that lists the values below the table. It can also get really busy, which makes the chart harder to read.

There are a number of choices about where to place your data labels if you choose to do so. The positions are not fixed.

Here are two options applied to a pie chart, inside end and outside end:

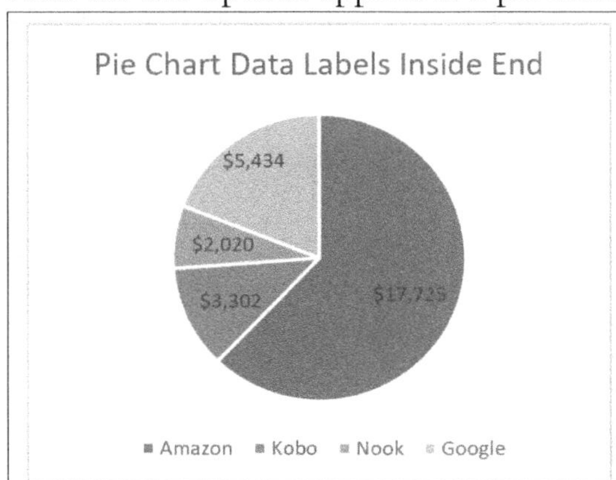

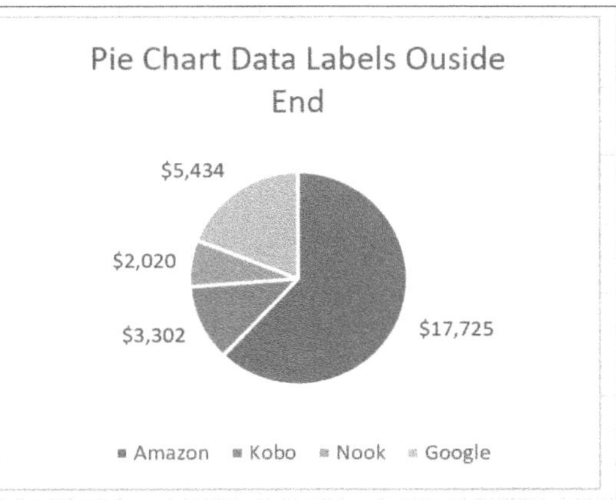

I prefer to have labels on the outside end. (Also, I'll show you how to do this later in the task pane, I tend to prefer to show the % value instead of the dollar value. You can show either one or both.)

You can also click and drag each text box to move them around.

Data Table

The data table option shows the data that created the chart in a table below it. Like here where you can see the dollar values for each store in each month below the columns that represent those values:

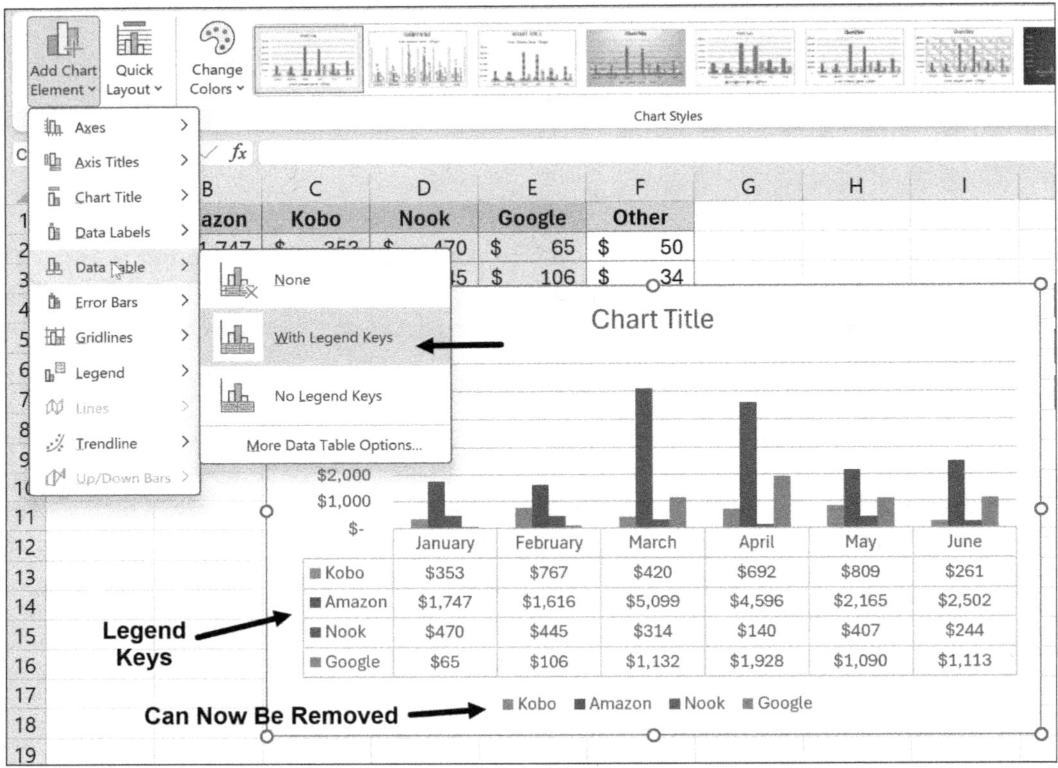

I often use this because I like to have the visual of the chart, but then I also like to see the actual numbers.

You can see that you have a choice to include legend keys or to leave them out. Above I included them. They show the color next to the store name in the data table. The nice thing about doing that is it lets you remove the legend as a separate element.

Error Bars

This option lets you add error bars to the results in your chart. The dropdown contains choices for standard error, percentage, and standard deviation and will apply to all of your category values. For example, with store in the column charts we looked at, you'd have one error bar for each store.

Choosing the More Error Bar Options will let you specify which category values to apply an error bar to. It will also open a Format Error Bars task pane with a custom and a fixed value option. The task pane allows you to control whether the bars go plus, minus, or both, and whether they have a cap at the end.

Gridlines

Gridlines can make it easier to read the data in a chart by providing lines in the background that a reader can follow to the axes to see the associated value.

You can add horizontal or vertical gridlines, and choose to include major lines and/or minor lines. Major lines have wider spacing between each line.

Legend

This option lets you choose where to place the legend (the guide that tells people what color corresponds to what label).

It can be on the top, bottom, left side, or right side. You can also manually position it if you need to as long as you add one.

It is also possible to remove the legend entirely, like I do when I use a data table with legend keys.

Lines

The lines option is available with line and area charts, and allows you to add drop lines and/or high-low lines.

Drop lines draw a vertical line from the top data point down to the horizontal axis.

High-low lines draw a vertical line from the top data point to the bottom data point for each entry.

Trendline

A trendline allows you to add a line onto your chart that either shows a linear or exponential trend based on the values in the chart, shows a linear forecast extrapolated from your values, or shows the moving average of your values.

When you click on this one, it will make you choose one of the values from your legend to create the line from.

The line it inserts will be a dotted line the same color as the category value you chose.

On the next page, for example, I've added trendlines for Amazon and Google:

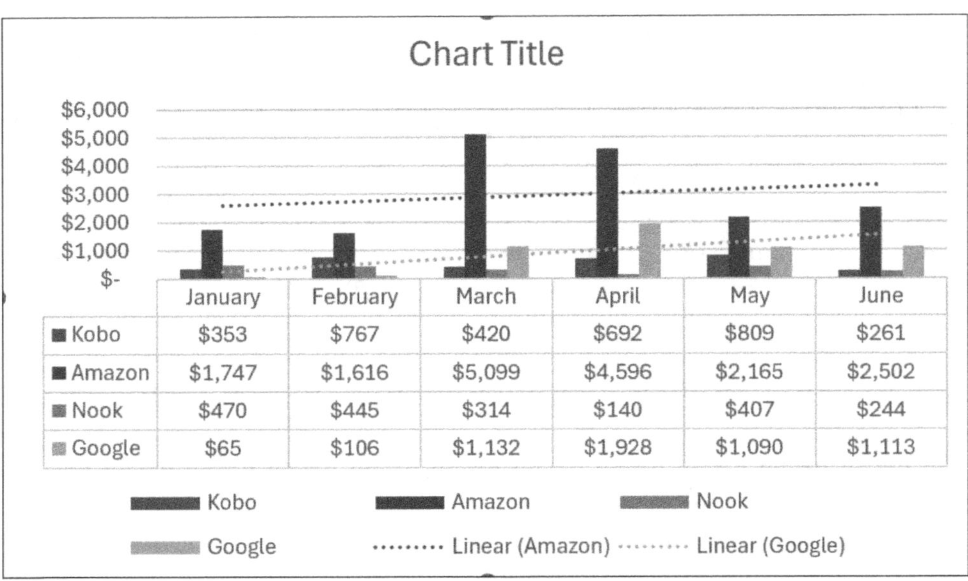

Make sure the type of trendline you choose makes sense for your data. Excel will apply whatever you tell it to, but sometimes the data doesn't justify that. A linear trendline, for example, is not a good choice to use with exponential data.

Up/Down Bars

Up/Down Bars are available for line charts. They draw a bar between two lines on the chart to show a visible change in the distance between the two from entry to entry.

* * *

Format Chart Area Task Pane

As I mentioned above, there is also a task pane option for formatting your chart.

You can open the task pane by double-clicking on your chart. Another option is to right-click on the chart and choose Format Chart Area from the dropdown menu.

You can also choose the More Options choice from any of the secondary dropdown menus for the chart elements.

Using the secondary dropdown menus is probably the best way to get you to the specific task pane you want to work with. You can always navigate there once the task pane is open, by using the dropdowns and icons at the top, but sometimes it's hard to know exactly where to go.

Here, for example, is the task pane that opens when I use the Data Labels secondary dropdown menu for a pie chart to choose More Data Label Options:

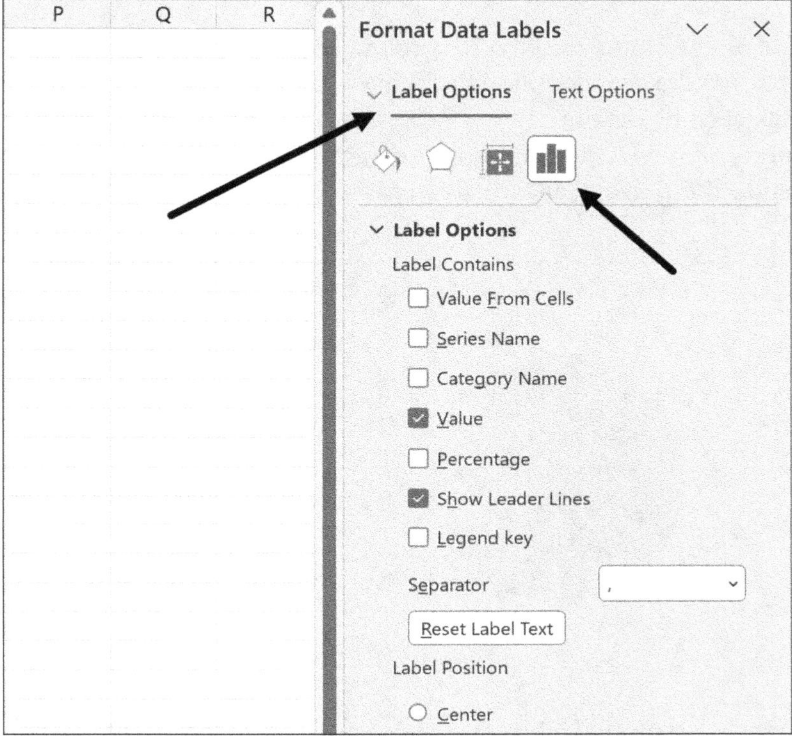

That brought me straight to where I can choose to show data labels as a percent. I could have also added data labels to the pie chart, opened the task pane, changed the top option to Series 1 Data Labels, and then clicked on the fourth icon for Label Options:

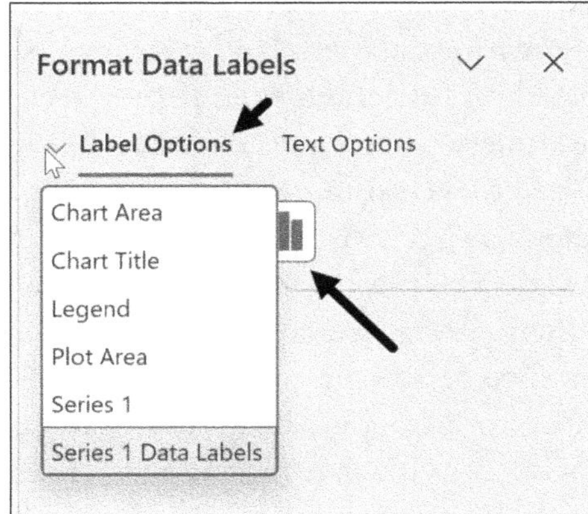

:

(You have to have already added data labels to use that dropdown in the task pane, though.)

Display Pie Chart Percent

The More Data Label Options task pane window (seen above) has a Label Contains section under Label Options. That section has checkboxes for Value, Percentage, and more. For a pie chart, Value is checked by default.

To include percent as well, just check the box for Percentage.

To only include the percent, like in this example, uncheck Value and check the box for Percentage.

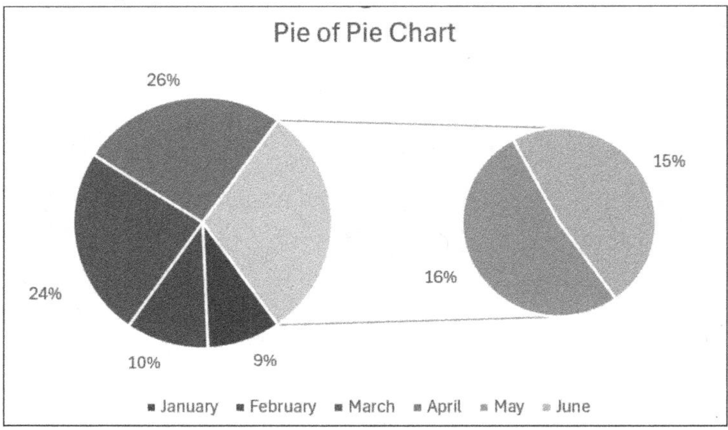

In the above chart I also deleted a box that showed 31% for the pie slice in the main pie chart that is broken out in the secondary chart. (You can do that by just clicking on a text box in the chart and using Delete.)

Leader Lines and Category Name

Two other choices there are Show Leader Lines and Category Name.

Leader lines should be turned on by default even if they aren't initially visible.

I like to have them, because they connect a data label to its element, so even if you have to move data labels around to make everything fit, you can still see what label goes to what element. (Just left-click and drag the text box for a data label to reposition it.)

On the next page, for example, is a pie chart with a lot of values where I had to move the data labels around to keep them from overlapping, and you can see the leader lines that connect each value back to its slice of the pie.

Note the other thing I chose to do here. I turned on Category Name for the data labels, too, so that a legend wasn't needed. With that many slices, trying to distinguish by color just doesn't work well.

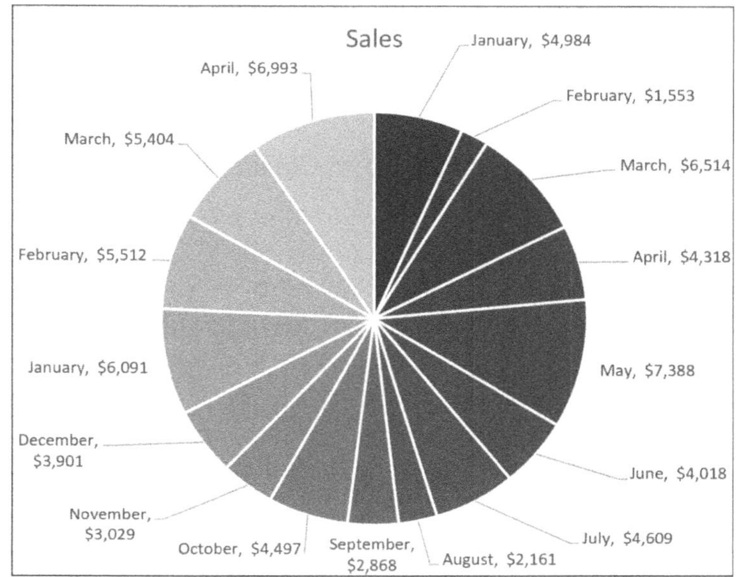

Explode Your Pie Chart

I sometimes like to "explode" a pie chart so that the various slices have space between them. That can be found by clicking on Series Options in the task pane dropdown, and then the third icon listed, which is also Series Options.

(If you can't find one of these settings, try clicking onto that element in your chart and then going to the task pane.)

The higher the percentage you input in the pie explosion box or choose using the slider, the more white space there will be between the various slices of the pie:

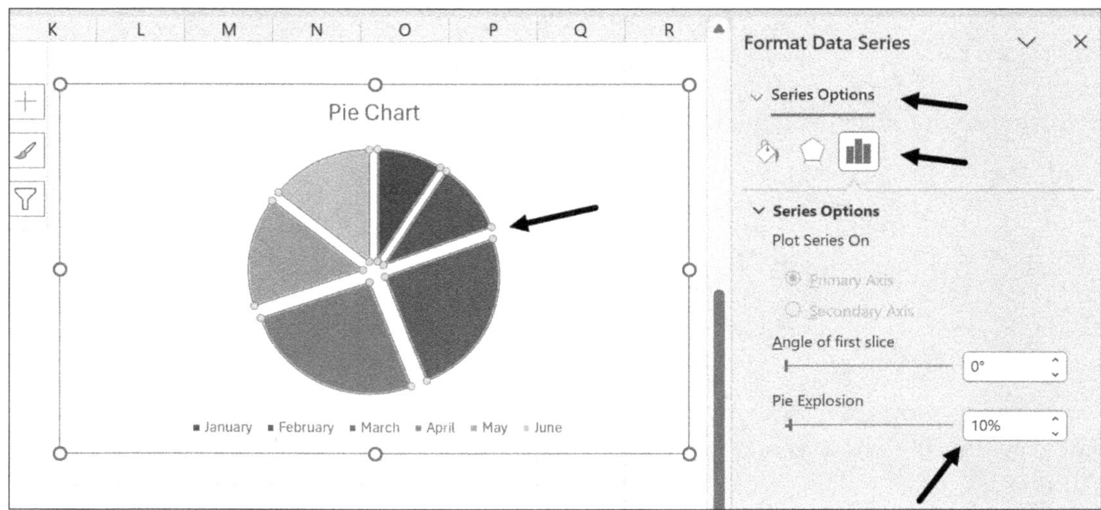

Rotate Your Pie Chart

You can also rotate your pie chart to control which slice is where. To do that, play with the Angle of First Slice setting also located in the Series Options section of the task pane.

Customize Your Histogram

The chart task pane is also the only way I know to customize the size of each histogram bin and the range of values used.

For this one you want Horizontal Axis, Axis Options.

The default is Automatic, but you can specify either the bin width or the number of bins instead.

You can also set the minimum and maximum values using the overflow and underflow bin fields. For example, here I have a range of 10 to 50 with five total bins. Anything under 10 gets dumped into the first bin, anything over 50 gets dumped into the last one. The three in between cover equal ranges of 13.33 each:

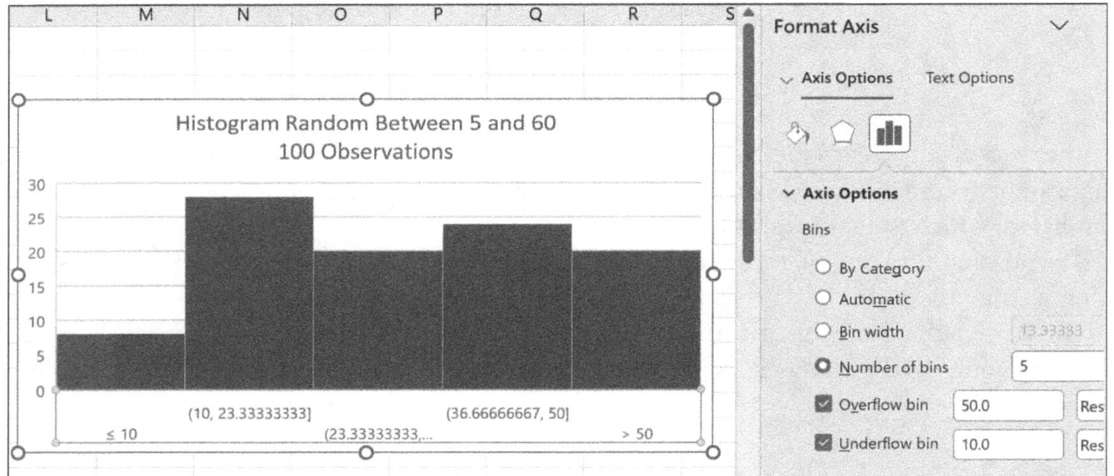

For this one, your chart will update when you click away from the task pane.

* * *

Finally, a few quick points on moving elements or charts around.

Move a Chart

If you need to move the whole chart, left-click and drag. Just be sure not to click on a specific element within the chart or you'll end up moving the element instead. (Remember, Ctrl + Z to Undo.)

You can also select a chart and use Ctrl + X to cut or Ctrl + C to copy, and then go to another worksheet, Word document, or PowerPoint presentation, and use Ctrl + V to paste. (Or your preferred method to copy/cut and paste, I just like the control shortcuts.)

Move or Resize a Chart Element

As I've mentioned a few times already, it is possible to move a chart element around, too. I often move data labels, for example. Just click on that element and drag.

But be aware that sometimes it may not work. I was just struggling to move the chart title on a histogram. I was able to do so just fine on other chart types, but for some reason histograms weren't cooperating with me.

When you click on a chart element that can be edited, there will be white circles at each corner and in the middle of each side that you can left-click and drag to resize. When you resize an element, all of the contents of that element—like the text within a legend—should also resize.

If you don't see white circles, but only blue ones at the corners, you should be able to move that element when your cursor has arrows pointing in four directions by left-clicking and dragging, but you won't be able to resize it.

In general, I don't find I need to manually move or resize elements in charts often. It's more that I accidentally do so sometimes when trying to move the whole chart around. Just remember that Ctrl + Z will undo any mistake you make with a chart.

Pivot Charts

Now that we've finished our discussion of charts, let's circle back to pivot tables, because it is possible to create a chart from data in a pivot table.

The first step is to build the pivot table that has the information you want to use in your chart.

Next, click on your pivot table, and either go to the Tools section of the PivotTable Analyze tab, or to the Charts section of the Insert tab. Both have a PivotChart option.

Click on the PivotChart icon to bring up an Insert Chart dialogue box:

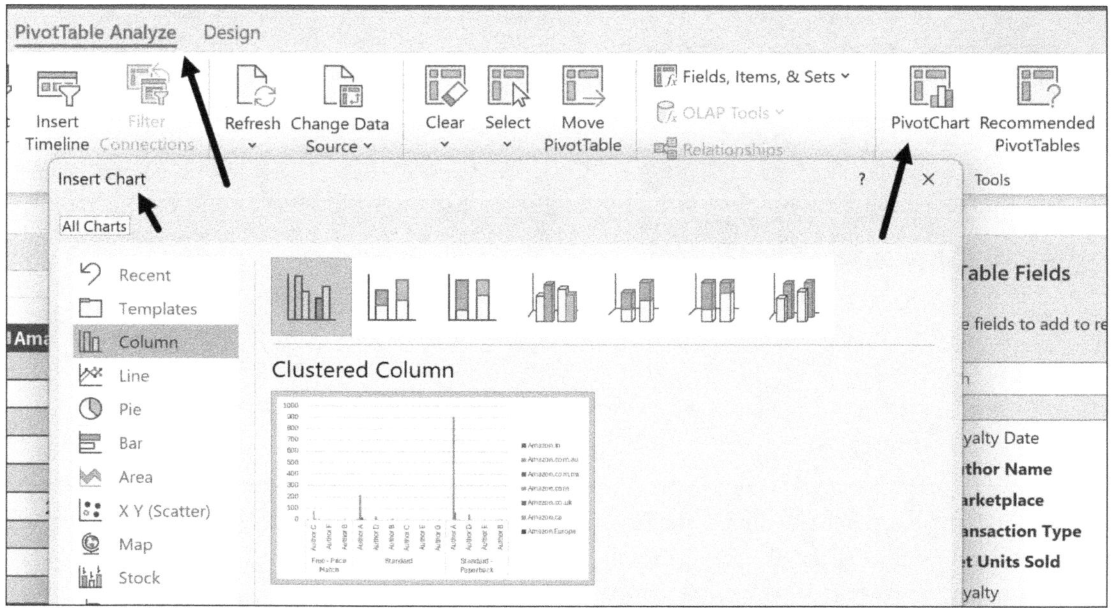

The preview for each chart type will show what your chart will look like given the data in the pivot table. Click on the chart type you want, and then click OK.

The pivot chart that Excel creates will be more dynamic than a standard chart:

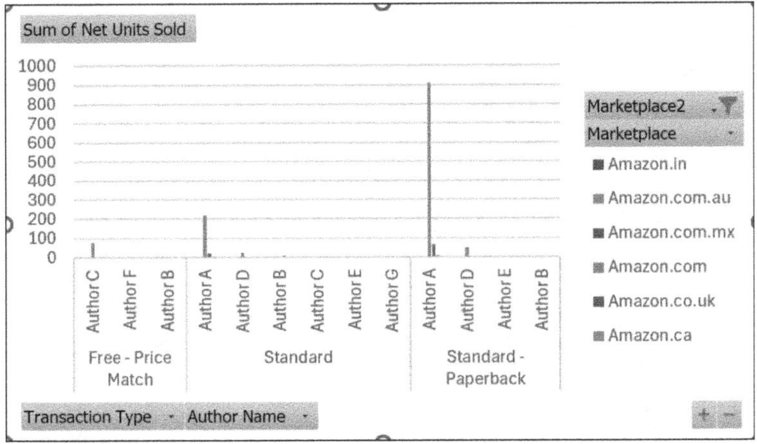

Each of the gray fields that you see in the chart above is a field from the pivot table. The ones that are being used to build the axes—in this case, transaction type, author name, and marketplace (with two levels because I have a group for Amazon Europe)—can be filtered right there in the chart.

Here, for example, I used the Marketplace dropdown and chose to only display results for Amazon Europe:

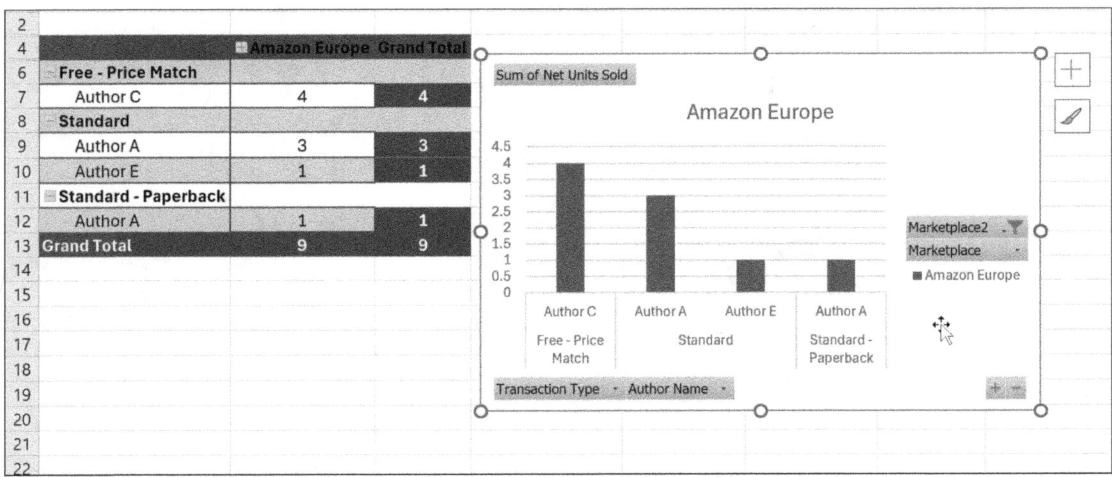

	Amazon Europe	Grand Total
Free - Price Match		
Author C	4	4
Standard		
Author A	3	3
Author E	1	1
Standard - Paperback		
Author A	1	1
Grand Total	9	9

Note what happened to the pivot table in the background when I did that. It automatically updated based on the filters I applied to the chart.

It is important to realize that this connection exists. Because any changes you make to the pivot table will change your pivot chart, and any changes you make to the pivot chart will change your pivot table.

Also, I found that sometimes I needed to go to the pivot chart and update my filters there to see the full data in my pivot table.

If you ever create a pivot chart and you want to "lock it in" so that it can't be impacted by changes you make to the pivot table, you can copy the chart and then paste it special as a picture.

That will lock it in as is. You won't be able to edit it ever.

In terms of formatting your pivot chart, it basically works the same as a normal chart in terms of using the Design and Format tabs or the task pane. Just keep in mind that something like "switch row/column" will also be reflected in your pivot table. It will flip your entries from Rows to Columns and Columns to Rows.

I have found pivot charts particularly useful for things like isolating one value at a time. For example, we've been working with data here that covers different authors or different stores. With a pivot chart, I can use the filter functionality in the chart to quickly show me a chart for each author or each store. Doing that with a standard chart would be much more time-consuming.

Appendix A: Basic Terminology

Workbook

A workbook is what Excel likes to call an Excel file.

Worksheet

Excel defines a worksheet as the primary document you use in Excel to store and work with your data. A worksheet is organized into Columns and Rows that form Cells. A workbook can contain multiple worksheets.

Columns

Excel uses columns and rows to display information. Columns run across the top of the worksheet and, unless you've done something funky with your settings, are identified using letters of the alphabet.

The first column in a worksheet will always be Column A. And the number of columns in your worksheet will remain the same, regardless of how many columns you delete, add, or move around. Think of columns as location information that is actually separate from the data in the worksheet.

Rows

Rows run down the side of each worksheet and are numbered starting at 1 and up to a very high number. Row numbers are also locational information. The first row will always be numbered 1, the second row will always be numbered 2, and so on and so forth. There will also always be a fixed number of rows in each worksheet regardless of how many rows of data you delete, add, or move around.

Cells

Cells are where the row and column data comes together. Cells are identified using the letter for the column and the number for the row that intersect to form that cell. For example, Cell A1 is the cell that is in the first column and first row of the worksheet.

Click

If I tell you to click on something, that means to use your mouse (or trackpad) to move the cursor on the screen over to a specific location and left-click or right-click on the option. If you left-click, this selects the item. If you right-click, this generally displays a dropdown list of options to choose from. If I don't tell you which to do, left- or right-click, then left-click.

Left-click/Right-click

If you look at your mouse you generally have two flat buttons to press. One is on the left side, one is on the right. If I say left-click that means to press down on the button on the left. If I say right-click that means press down on the button on the right.

Select

If I tell you to "select" cells, that means to highlight them. You can either left-click and drag to select a range of cells or hold down the Ctrl key as you click on individual cells. To select an entire column, click on the letter for the column. To select an entire row, click on the number for the row.

Data

Data is the information you enter into your worksheet.

Data Table

I may also sometimes refer to a data table or table of data. This is just a combination of cells that contain data in them.

Arrow

If I tell you to arrow to somewhere or to arrow right, left, up, or down, this just means use the arrow keys to navigate to a new cell.

Cursor Functions

The cursor is what moves around when you move your mouse or use the trackpad. In Excel the cursor changes its appearance depending on what functions you can perform.

Tab

I am going to talk a lot about Tabs, which are the options you have to choose from at the top of the workspace. The default tab names are File, Home, Insert, Page Layout, Formulas, Data, Review, View, and Help. But there are certain times when additional tabs will appear, for example, when you create a pivot table or a chart.

(This should not be confused with the Tab key which can be used to move across cells.)

Dropdown Menus

A dropdown menu is a listing of available choices that you can see when you right-click in certain places such as the main workspace or on a worksheet name. You will also see them when you click on an arrow next to or below an option in the top menu.

Dialogue Boxes

Dialogue boxes are pop-up boxes that contain additional choices.

Scroll Bars

When you have more information than will show in a screen, dialogue box, or dropdown menu, you will see scroll bars on the right side or bottom that allow you to navigate to see the rest of the information.

Formula Bar

The formula bar is the long white bar at the top of the main workspace directly below the top menu options that lets you see the actual contents of a cell, not just the displayed value.

Cell Notation

Cells are referred to by their column and row position. So Cell A1 is the cell that's the intersection of the first column and first row in the worksheet.

When written in Excel you just use A1, you do not need to include the word cell. A colon (:) can be used to reference a range of cells. A comma (,) can be used to separate cell references.

When in doubt about how to define a cell range, click into a cell, type =, and then go and select the cells you want to reference. Excel will describe your selection in the formula bar using cell notation.

Paste Special Values

Paste Special Values is a way of pasting copied values that keeps the calculation results or the cell values but removes any formulas or formatting.

Task Pane

On occasion Excel will open a task pane, which is different from a dialogue box because it is part of the workspace. These will normally appear on the right-hand side in Excel for tasks such as working with pivot tables or charts or using the built-in Help function. (They often appear on the left-hand side in Word.)

They can be closed by clicking on the X in the top right corner.

About the Author

M.L. Humphrey is a former stockbroker with a degree in Economics from Stanford and an MBA from Wharton who has spent close to twenty years as a regulator and consultant in the financial services industry.

You can reach M.L. at mlhumphreywriter@gmail.com or at mlhumphrey.com.

* * *

If you want to learn more about Microsoft Excel, check out *Excel Tips and Tricks* or one of the main Excel 2024 Essentials titles, *Excel 2024 for Beginners*, *Intermediate Excel 2024*, or *Excel 2024 Useful Functions.*

www.ingramcontent.com/pod-product-compliance
Lightning Source LLC
LaVergne TN
LVHW081349050326
832903LV00024B/1371